THE SKELETAL SYSTEM

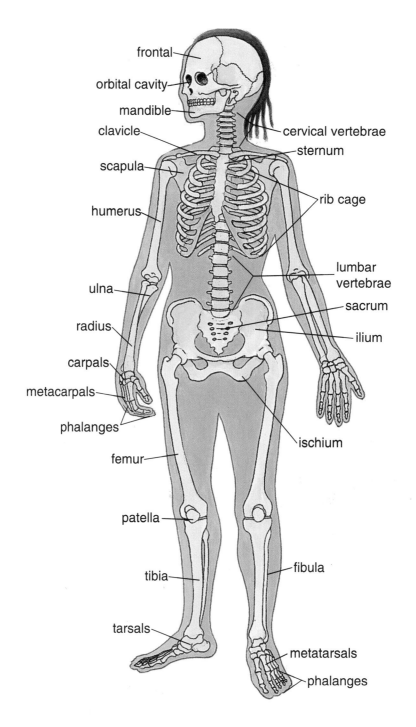

frontal
orbital cavity
mandible
clavicle
scapula
humerus
ulna
radius
carpals
metacarpals
phalanges
femur
patella
tibia
tarsals

cervical vertebrae
sternum
rib cage
lumbar vertebrae
sacrum
ilium
ischium
fibula
metatarsals
phalanges

The Skeletal System

HUMAN
BODY
SYSTEMS

THE
SKELETAL
SYSTEM

Dr. Alvin, Virginia, and Robert Silverstein

TWENTY-FIRST CENTURY BOOKS
A Division of Henry Holt and Company
New York

Twenty-First Century Books
A Division of Henry Holt and Company, Inc.
115 West 18th Street
New York, NY 10011

Henry Holt ® and colophon are trademarks of
Henry Holt and Company, Inc.
Publishers since 1866

Library of Congress Cataloging-in-Publication Data
Silverstein, Alvin.
Skeletal system / Alvin, Virginia, and Robert Silverstein.—1st ed.
p.   cm. — (Human body systems)
Includes index.
1. Musculoskeletal system—Juvenile literature. 2. Skeleton—Juvenile literature. [1. Skeleton.
2. Bones.] I. Silverstein, Virginia B. II. Silverstein, Robert A. III. Title. IV. Series.
QP301.S55 1994
612.7'5—dc20   94-21421
                                                                                       CIP
                                                                                       AC

ISBN 0-8050-2837-4
First Edition 1994

Printed in Mexico
All first editions are printed on acid-free paper ∞.
10 9 8 7 6 5 4 3 2 1

Drawings by Lloyd Birmingham

Photo Credits

cover: Howard Sochurek/The Stock Market
p. 8: Karl Maslowski/Photo Researchers, Inc.; p. 11: Tom McHugh/Steinhart Aquarium/Photo
Researchers, Inc.; p. 13: Tom McHugh/Photo Researchers, Inc.; p. 16(l): Mark Marten/National
Library of Medicine/Photo Researchers, Inc.; p. 16(r): Science Photo Library/Photo Researchers,
Inc.; p. 17: Mark Marten/National Library of Medicine/Photo Researchers, Inc.; pp. 18, 21, and
63: Biophoto Associates/Photo Researchers, Inc.; pp. 22 and 24: CRNI/Science Photo
Library/Photo Researchers, Inc.; p. 29: Jean-Yves Ruszniewski/Agence Vandystadt/Photo
Researchers, Inc.; p. 35: NASA/Science Source/Photo Researchers, Inc.; p. 36: A. Sieveking/Petit
Format/Photo Researchers, Inc.; p. 39: Will and Deni McIntyre/Photo Researchers, Inc.; p. 41(l):
Ken Eward/Science Source/Photo Researchers, Inc.; 41(r): Don Fawcett/E. Shelton/Science
Source/Photo Researchers, Inc.; p. 55: Dave Roberts/Science Photo Library/Photo Researchers,
Inc.; p. 62: M. Abbey/Photo Researchers, Inc.; p. 66: Alfred Pasieka/Science Photo
Library/Photo Researchers, Inc.; p. 67: Richard T. Nowitz/Photo Researchers, Inc.; p. 70: NASA;
p. 74: Dept. of Clinical Radiology, Salisbury District Hospital/Science Photo Library/Photo
Researchers, Inc.; p. 76: Sue Ford/Science Photo Library/Photo Researchers, Inc.; p. 80: Scott
Camazine/Science Source/Photo Researchers, Inc.; p. 82: Catherine Ursillo/Photo Researchers,
Inc.; p. 88: John Reader/Science Photo Library/Photo Researchers, Inc.

CONTENTS

SECTION 1

FRAMEWORKS FOR LIFE

Have you ever set up a tent? First you have to get the tent poles in place. They will act as a framework to support the canvas tent and give it shape. The house you live in also has an inner framework. It may be made of wooden beams nailed together. Or perhaps you live in a big apartment house that has a framework of steel girders. Cars and buses, boats and airplanes all have an inner framework that helps to support them and hold their basic shape.

Your body, too, has an inner framework. It is called the skeleton, and it is made of bones. You can feel the hard bones in your fingers. Or squeeze your arms and legs, or press down on the top of your head. There are firm bones under the skin in nearly all parts of your body. Without this inner framework, your body would collapse like a tent whose poles were knocked over.

Dogs and cats, mice and elephants, frogs and snakes all have skeletons made of bones very much like ours. In all these animals the skeleton is an inner framework, covered by layers of soft flesh.

Many members of the animal kingdom have a different kind of skeleton—a skeleton on the outside. Insects and spiders, lobsters and crayfish all have an outer skeleton made like a jointed suit of armor. Clams and snails have hard limy shells that form a framework on the outside.

The shell of a snail, like the framework of a house, is a very solid structure. It cannot bend back and forth.

A crayfish

But the skeletons of most living things are very flexible. Bend your arm, roll your head about, curl your fingers into a ball and then stretch them.

Bones themselves are rather hard. Why isn't the skeleton stiff and rigid like the framework of a house? The flexibility comes from the way the bones are put together. The beams of a house are all nailed firmly together. Bones are held in place by bands of tough tissues called **ligaments** and **tendons**. These connections permit the bones to move about with some freedom.

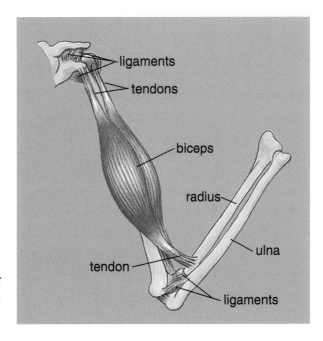

Ligaments and tendons hold bones together and give the skeleton flexibility.

How does a bone move? Bones cannot move by themselves. They are pulled by muscles. Indeed, muscles not only move bones, but they also help to keep them in the proper positions when they are not moving. The wooden frame of a house provides the support for the walls and floors and roof, but the bones of the body do not provide all the support for the skin and for the soft tissues and organs inside us. It is the bones and muscles together that provide support for our bodies.

ANIMAL SKELETONS

A bird's wing and an insect's wing are both used for flying. But these wings are constructed very differently. The bird's wing is made of flesh, with a rich supply of blood vessels. It has an inner framework of bone, which is attached to the rest of its skeleton in much the same way that your arm bones are attached to the rest of your skeleton. The insect's wings are made of a thin membrane, stretched across a network of wirelike structures. It is built rather like a kite. It does not contain any blood vessels or bones. Scientists have learned a lot about how animals are related by studying the way their skeletons are constructed.

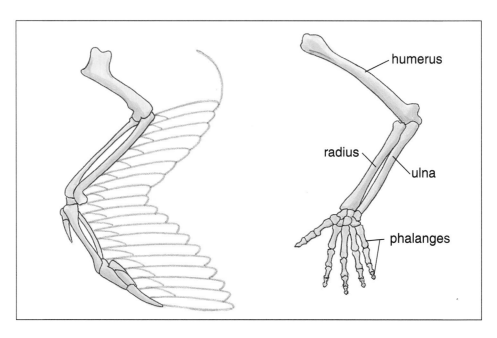

A bird's wing has an inner framework of bones that are similar to the bones of a human arm, wrist, and hand.

When scientists classify animals they divide them into two groups, depending on the type of skeleton they have. Humans and other mammals, birds, reptiles, and fish all have a **backbone**, or **spine**, which is a row of bones down their backs. The backbone supports the rest of the skeleton. Animals with a backbone are called **vertebrates**. (Each of the bones in the spine is called a vertebra.)

Insects, shellfish, and jellyfish do not have a backbone. They are called **invertebrates**. Some invertebrates, such as crabs, lobsters, and insects, have their skeletons on the outside of their bodies. This outer shell, or casing, gives the animal its shape. Scientists call this kind of body framework an **exoskeleton**.

Some invertebrates, such as jellyfish and earthworms, have no hard skeleton at all. Their shape and form can change. In fact, they move by changing the shape of their bodies.

A jellyfish has no backbone.

A SKELETON MADE OF WATER

An earthworm is divided into many sections. It moves by using muscles that are attached to its skin. This skin is much softer than the hard exoskeleton of an insect, but the pressure of the fluid inside the earthworm's body makes its skin firm. So it has what scientists call a hydrostatic skeleton. (*Hydro-* means "water.") Water flows freely, but no matter how hard you squeeze it, you can't force it to take up less space. If you squeeze a water-filled balloon, the part you are squeezing gets smaller, but it bulges out somewhere else. When an earthworm's muscles pull on its skin, some sections of its body get shorter and fatter while others get longer and thinner. So by stretching out and then bracing itself with the thicker parts of its body the worm can wriggle along.

EXOSKELETONS

An insect's outer covering is a lot like the suits of armor that were worn by knights in the Middle Ages. It is hard and tough and protects the insect from injury. And it is made of many plates, joined together and molded to the shape of the insect's body. If it were not for the many joints in its exoskeleton, an insect would not be able to move at all. Its "armor" covering would keep it rigidly in place like a statue.

An insect's exoskeleton is called the **cuticle**. It is made of a substance called **chitin**, produced by the insect's skin cells. A medieval knight's metal armor was so heavy that he had to be lifted up onto his horse. But the chitin that forms an insect's "armor" is more like plastic—lightweight and flexible but very tough. In parts of the insect's cuticle that do not need to be flexible, proteins form a tough, leathery substance something like your fingernails. In the joints, a rubbery substance makes the cuticle extra flexible. The cuticle is covered with an outer layer of wax that makes it like a waterproof raincoat and also helps to keep the insect from losing moisture from its body.

The cuticle covers every part of the insect's body, and even lines some of its internal organs. Muscles attached to the inside of the insect's chitin skeleton help it move. When the muscles shorten, or contract, body segments are pulled toward other segments, folding in at the joints between the segments.

An exoskeleton allows much faster and stronger movements than an earthworm's hydrostatic skeleton. But it has some disadvantages. A protective shell can sometimes be too heavy to handle. Have you ever seen a beetle on its back, kicking wildly as it tries to turn itself over? Very few insects are larger than an inch or two; if they grew much bigger, their exoskeletons would be too thick and heavy.

Lobsters and crabs are crustaceans, close relatives of the insects, and their bodies are also covered with a cuticle. This cuticle is made into a hard shell by deposits of calcium salts (lime). These animals can grow larger than insects because they are water animals. The water's buoyancy helps to support their weight.

Another disadvantage of an exoskeleton is that insects and crustaceans soon grow too big for their outer covering—and there is no way to make it larger. Instead, a new cuticle forms underneath the old one, which finally splits and falls away. This shedding of the old exoskeleton is called **molting**. But the new cuticle is soft at first. It takes a few hours to harden, and during that time insects and crustaceans are without their protective armor.

This tarantula has just shed the exoskeleton it outgrew.

Snails and clams also have a limy outer shell that protects and supports the soft tissues of their bodies. But they can grow without molting. As they grow, they simply add more shell around the outer edge of the old one.

INTERNAL SKELETONS

In many ways, an internal skeleton, called an **endoskeleton**, is even better than an exoskeleton. The animal can move around with much greater ease, without losing much in the way of strength, because bones provide a hard, firm surface to anchor muscles.

All vertebrates share a similar skeletal plan. First there is an **axial skeleton**, which runs lengthwise down the center of the body. It consists of the skull, the backbone, and the ribs. The **appendicular skeleton** is made up of the bones that support the appendages—the arms, legs, fins, or wings. *Appendicular* comes from a word meaning "to hang," and the appendicular skeleton "hangs from," or is attached to, the axial skeleton.

The inner structure of the vertebrates is amazingly similar. Most backboned animals have a pair of front limbs and a pair of hind limbs. Even snakes and whales, which do not have legs, have skeletons that include hip and leg bones similar to those of many other vertebrates. A giraffe's neck has the same number of bones as a mouse's neck, but the bones are bigger.

The skeletons of vertebrates are made of bones. Bones are hard but light. They contain both living and nonliving parts. A land animal's bones are all firmly connected to each other to support the weight of its body. But this is not necessary in vertebrates that live in the water, because the water provides part of the support. That is why, when you eat a fish, there seem to be so many bones that are not connected to each other.

Although a vertebrate's main feature is its endoskeleton, vertebrates have body parts that can move without using bones. Your intestines, for example, push food along in a series of muscle contractions called peristalsis, and your heart will continue to pump blood through your body all your life. These body parts use a hydrostatic skeleton. Muscles in the heart transfer the force of their contractions to the fluid (blood) that fills the heart and blood vessels. Muscles in the intestinal walls apply their force to the soupy food in the digestive tract. Vertebrates also make use of a sort of exoskeleton. When you are scared, the hairs on your body stand up in goose bumps. The muscles that raise the hairs use the hair shafts as an exoskeleton to exert their force against.

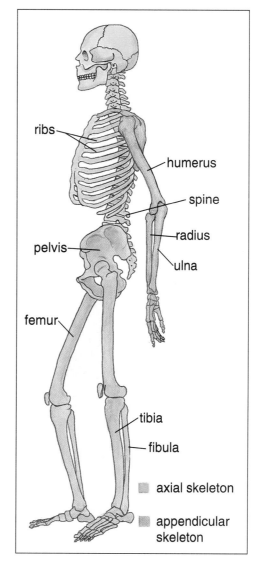

The human skeleton provides a framework for upright posture.

DID YOU KNOW THAT YOU HAVE TAILBONES?

The fused vertebrae at the end of your spine, called the coccyx, are similar to the tailbones of lizards, mice, and other animals with tails.

LEARNING ABOUT THE SKELETAL SYSTEM

For thousands of years people did not really understand much about how our bodies worked. But they knew bones were important. They could feel the bones beneath their skin, and they saw the bones inside animals and people that had died. When a person or animal died, the bones remained long after the rest of the body had disappeared. For this reason, in many cultures, people thought bones had magical powers.

One of the first things that people learned about bones was that broken bones could grow together again. When an arm or leg was broken, splints of wood were tied to it to keep the bones in place. However, sometimes the bones healed crookedly. The ancient Greeks invented mechanical devices to help bring broken bones back into line.

During the Middle Ages in Europe, the work of the second-century Greek physician Galen was regarded as the authority on the human body. But Galen had observed mainly animals, and some of his ideas of human anatomy were wrong. Very few accurate and detailed studies were made until the Renaissance, when artists began to focus on the beauty of the human body. The fifteenth-century genius Leonardo da Vinci made many precise drawings of the human skeleton, based on careful dissections of bodies, and showed how the bones worked with muscles to produce movements.

In the mid-sixteenth century, Andreas Vesalius, a Belgian scientist, wrote the first book about the anatomy of the human body. His book included detailed

Galen

Leonardo da Vinci

Andreas Vesalius

illustrations. One of them, showing a skeleton posed as though it were thinking about a skull lying on the table in front of it, may have inspired the famous graveyard scene in Shakespeare's play *Hamlet*.

Giovanni Alfonso Borelli, a seventeenth-century Italian scientist, showed that bones were like mechanical levers that are powered by muscles. He described the way bones and muscles worked in the body in mathematical terms. He also suggested that a physical reaction caused the muscles to contract when the brain sends them messages through nerves.

An eighteenth-century Italian scientist named Luigi Galvani discovered that a dead frog's leg moved when it was touched with a machine that produced an electric spark. Galvani believed that the physical reaction in us that caused muscles to contract was some kind of electrical power. Later scientists found that the brain does indeed send electrical messages through the nervous system. These electrical impulses tell the muscles to tighten or relax, which causes the muscles to move the bones of the skeleton.

Meanwhile, other medical researchers were studying the structure and growth of bone. Late in the seventeenth century, the English scientist Clopton Havers discovered channels running along the shafts of the long bones. These channels are still called Haversian canals in his honor.

In 1763 an English surgeon, John Belchier, measured bone growth by adding dye to the diet of animals. Another Englishman, William Hunter, studied cartilage, the gristly substance on the ends of bones. His brother, John Hunter, was the first to demonstrate that bone is a living tissue, which can grow and change.

The discovery of X rays in 1895, by the German physicist Wilhelm Roentgen, led to a revolution in the study of bones and the treatment of skeletal disorders. In X-ray photographs, the outlines of the bones could be clearly seen right through the body tissues covering them.

THE HUMAN SKELETON

Did you know that you have more bones than your mother or father? Each of them has 206 bones. But you have dozens more—and you had even more when you were younger. A newborn baby may have as many as 150 more bones than an adult!

Bones do not disappear as you grow older. Indeed, some new bones appear. But meanwhile, many of the bones of your body grow together, or fuse, to form a single bone where there were two or more.

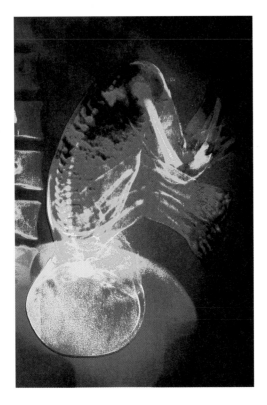

In this X ray of a fetus, the skeleton is clearly visible. At this stage of development, a good deal of the skeleton is composed of cartilage.

The bony framework of an adult weighs about 20 pounds (9 kilograms). Each of the 206 bones of the adult skeleton has its own name. The largest is the femur, or thighbone. It makes up one quarter of a person's height. The stirrup inside the ear is the smallest bone in the body—it is only 0.1 of an inch (0.25 centimeter) long.

When children draw a "stick figure" to represent a person, they are demonstrating a basic understanding of the skeletal structure that gives us our shape. The center of our skeleton is the skull and spine, which are each made up of a number of bones. Attached to this axial skeleton are two main "hangers," or girdles on which the bones that make up our arms and legs are suspended. The arms are attached to the **shoulder girdle** and the legs to the **pelvic girdle**. These limb girdles are large, wide, strong bones that can take a lot of strain, for example, when we lift heavy objects.

As the words of a popular song explain, each bone in the body is connected to another bone. Only the hyoid bone in the throat, which supports the tongue, is not attached to any other bone.

The skull is the top of our skeleton. The bones of the skull protect the brain and form the shape of the face. The skull sits on top of the spinal column. You can feel the small bones that make up the spinal column as it runs down your back. The spinal column protects the spinal cord, the main bundle of nerves that allows the brain to communicate with the rest of the body. At the top of the spinal column are the shoulder bones, which are connected to the arm bones, which in turn attach to the hand bones.

Twelve bones called the ribs curve around from each side of the spine to the front of the chest, forming the **rib cage**. The ribs help protect important body organs such as the heart and lungs. The spinal column runs down between the hips. Wide, curved bones stick out at the hips, forming the pelvis. The legs are attached to the pelvis, and the feet are attached to the leg bones.

The places where bones connect are called **joints**. The bones are held together and connected to muscles with special connective tissues called ligaments and tendons.

WHAT ARE BONES?

The word *skeleton* comes from the Greek for "dried up," but bones are not really as dry as rocks. In fact, bones are one-third water. They contain both living and nonliving parts. Minerals make the bones hard and strong, but they are not alive. Bone cells make the skeleton a living framework. Bones have blood and nerves inside, and they grow and change.

Bones are covered everywhere except at the joints by a thin white membrane called the **periosteum**. (*Periosteum* is Latin for "surrounding the bone.") This layer contains living cells that help in the growth and repair of bones. It also contains blood vessels and nerves.

Beneath the periosteum is the hard part of bone, called **compact bone**. Compact bone is so hard that surgeons have to cut it with a saw. Through tiny holes in this layer, nerves and blood vessels pass inside the bone.

Inside the layer of compact bone is a lacy network of bone with many small spaces inside. It looks rather like the cut edge of a sponge. This kind of bone is called spongy bone, or **cancellous bone**. (*Cancellous* comes from a Latin word that means "covered with bars.") Cancellous bone is nearly as strong as compact bone, but it is much lighter because part of it is just empty space.

In the center of some bones there is a jellylike substance called **bone marrow**. Bone marrow produces red blood cells, which carry oxygen through the bloodstream, white blood cells that fight infection, and blood platelets that help us to stop bleeding when we are cut.

Bone seems nonliving, like a stone. And indeed, part of the bone, called the **matrix**, is made of nonliving substances. It contains a mineral part: a type of calcium phosphate, a salt containing the elements calcium and phosphorus. Bone matrix also contains protein fibers. These fibers are nonliving, like the proteins in your hair and nails. When you cut your fingernails or hair, you do not bleed or feel anything. But if you could cut a very thin slice of bone and look at it under a microscope, you would see numerous living bone cells, called **osteocytes**, embedded between layers of hard bony tissue. (The name *osteocyte* comes from words meaning "bone" and "cell.")

The bony substance itself is arranged in long cylinders, nested one inside another. These groups of cylinders are called Haversian systems. The osteocytes are found in small hollows between the bony cylinders, and there is a hollow central channel in the middle of the smallest cylinder. This central channel is called a **Haversian canal**. Within the Haversian canal is one or more blood vessels. Bone cells, like all other living cells, need a constant supply of oxygen and food materials, which are carried to them in the bloodstream. Side branches of blood vessels cut through the covering of the bone.

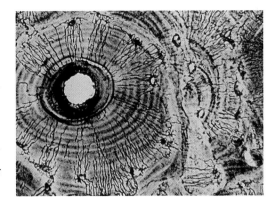

A Haversian canal is seen here in the left side of the photograph. Haversian canals are found in the middle of the smallest bony cylinders and carry blood vessels to the bone cells.

Though bones are all made of the same basic substance, they come in many different sizes and shapes. Bones are usually divided into four groups: long, short, flat, and irregular.

Long bones are found in the extremities. They are usually rodlike with knobby ends. They may be very big, such as the femur, or small like the bones in the little toe. Short bones, such as those in the wrist and ankles, are cube-shaped. Flat bones are two plates of compact bone that enclose a layer of spongy bone like a sandwich. The ribs, the shoulder blades, the breastbone, and most of the bones of the skull are flat bones. Irregular bones are a catchall category that includes the vertebrae, the bones of the inner ear, and other bones that do not fit into the other groups.

WHY ARE BONES SO STRONG?

Bones are almost as tough as cast iron or reinforced concrete but are much lighter. They are stronger than most synthetic materials. Indeed, one of the important problems researchers had to solve in designing artificial replacements for bones damaged so badly in accidents that they could not be repaired was to find strong enough materials. When they tried to make a stainless steel femur the same size as a normal femur made of bone, it snapped under the normal load of standing and walking. Special alloys had to be invented, and even they were not as good as the amazing natural substance, bone. Our leg bones can stand up to a force of one ton without snapping or bending.

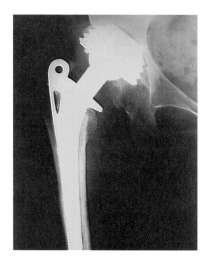

An X ray of an artificial hip showing a steel shaft (yellow) inserted into the femur

Why must bones be so strong? They have to hold up the weight of the body in normal activities, and they must also be able to withstand special emergency loads. When you jump down the steps or off a wall, you are putting a tremendous force on your leg bones when you land.

Bones are so strong and yet so light because of the way they are constructed. Bones contain a tough protein fiber called **collagen**. This name comes from Greek words *kolla,* meaning "glue," and *gen,* meaning "forming." On the collagen meshwork, mineral salts are deposited to make the final structure as strong as reinforced concrete. How does it get so strong? Calcium and phosphorus atoms are packed tightly together in crystalline patterns. Diamonds, which are the hardest natural substance, have a similar structure. Bone crumbles if collagen is removed, and if the salts are removed it becomes rubbery.

About 70 percent of an adult's bones are minerals. The other 30 percent is organic matter, which gives the bone flexibility. In babies this proportion is reversed.

Tendons are almost pure collagen. In cartilage, thin collagen fibers are embedded in a plasticlike polymer made of sugar units. The chitin in an insect's exoskeleton is also a sugar polymer.

MODELS OF BONES

You can make some models illustrating how the two parts of the bone matrix give bone its special properties. Take a piece of cheesecloth and roll it into a tube. Cheesecloth is a mesh of cotton fibers, much like the network of protein fibers in the bone matrix. The cheesecloth tube will not break easily, but it will quickly flatten out. It will not hold a firm shape.

Next, seal off one end of an empty cardboard tube from a roll of paper towels or toilet paper. Fill the tube with plaster of paris that has been mixed with water in the right proportions to make a plaster model. When the plaster hardens, peel off the cardboard mold. Now you have a plaster cylinder, something like a long bone. It is firm and rigid, but it is not very strong. You can break it easily, just by bending it with your hands.

Now place a roll of cheesecloth several layers thick inside another cardboard tube and fill that with plaster of paris. When the plaster sets, you will have a plaster rod that looks just like the other one but has layers of cheesecloth embedded inside. This rod will be much harder to break. The plaster gives it shape, and the network of fibers strengthens it.

TENDONS AND LIGAMENTS

Our bones are held together by connective tissue, much the way the parts of a wooden marionette are joined with string. There are three main types of connective tissue in the human skeletal system: cartilage, tendons, and ligaments. Microscopic fibers of the protein collagen add to the strength of these connective tissues, just as they strengthen bone. But the matrix of cartilage, tendons, and ligaments does not contain deposits of calcium salts so these tissues are not hard like bone.

Collagen fibers in this micrograph of connective tissue appear as orange bands.

Tendons connect muscles to bones. They are like tough cords that allow muscles to pull on bones. The ends of many muscles taper off into stringy tendons at each end. Look at the back of your hand while you move your fingers up and down. Narrow bands, running from the fingers to the wrist, are raised and lowered as your fingers move. These are tendons. A particularly large tendon just above your heel attaches the calf muscle to the heel bone. It is called the Achilles tendon. Tendons in the calf and arch stretch when we walk or run, then spring back into shape, decreasing the work the muscles have to do.

Bones are fastened to other bones by ligaments. Ligaments are like strong fibrous straps. Some ligaments are round like ropes. Others are flat like ribbons or bandages. They wrap around joints to hold bones together. (Their name comes from a word meaning "to tie.") Ligaments can stretch more than tendons and allow bones to move freely without coming apart. This makes a joint more stable. Ligaments hold the arm bones in place in the shoulder joints and

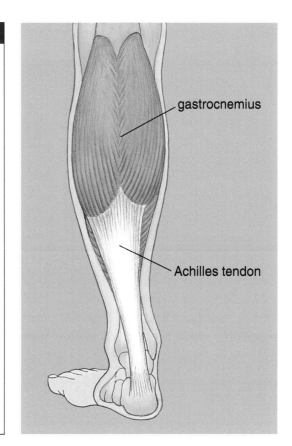

gastrocnemius

Achilles tendon

help to keep the knees sturdy. They hold many small bones together in the ankles and wrists. Shoelacelike ligaments reinforce the bones of the neck and vertebral column.

Cartilage is a flexible gristly, rubbery substance that supports bones and protects them from rubbing against each other. A developing baby's skeleton is actually made of cartilage, not bone. As the baby grows in the womb, a good deal of the cartilage hardens and becomes bone. After birth, real bone gradually replaces the remaining cartilage skeleton, but cartilage remains at the ends of bones.

JOINTS

Bones are very stiff and hard, but our bodies can bend and move because bones are fitted together in joints. These are connecting points where two or more bones are joined together. There are a number of different kinds of joints in the body.

Make a fist with one hand. Cup the fingers of the other hand around it. This is what a **ball-and-socket joint** looks like. You can turn the ball of your fist freely in any direction within the socket formed by the other hand. Ball-and-socket joints provide the most freedom of movement of any type of joint. The joints in your shoulders and hips are of this type. You can swing your arm or leg around in a full circle.

Another kind of joint is the **hinge joint**, which works something like the hinge of a door. Your knees, elbows, and knuckles have hinge joints. In fact, the knee joint is the biggest joint in the body. Hinge joints can move only back and forth.

Move your thumb back and forth. Now move it up and down, and around in a circle. What kind of a joint connects your thumb bones to your hand? You can move your thumb more freely than you can move the parts of your arms and legs connected at your elbow and knee joints, so it is not a hinge joint. Yet you do not have quite as much freedom as a ball-and-socket joint provides. The kind of joint that is found in your thumb is called a **saddle joint**, because it is shaped something like a saddle. It is because of this saddle joint in our thumb that we can pick up tiny objects such as needles. There is also a saddle joint in the wrist. Saddle joints in the ankles allow you to stand on your toes, or lean forward and backward.

At the top of the spinal column a **pivot joint** allows us to turn our head from side to side. **Gliding joints** between vertebrae in the spine allow only a small amount of movement as the two flat surfaces glide over each other.

Although each vertebral joint can move only slightly, together their gliding movements permit us to twist and bend.

Some joints do not permit any movement at all. The bones of your skull are held together in firm, immovable joints called **sutures**. Can you feel any of them? How many of your joints can you find?

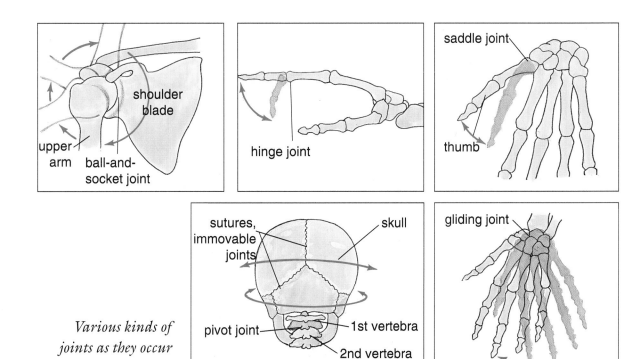

Various kinds of joints as they occur in the human body

Some people say they are "double-jointed" because they can bend their fingers very far back or perform amazing contortions. However, they don't really have extra joints. People who are "double-jointed" can move in ways most people can't because the ligaments holding their joints together can stretch farther than normal, which allows the bones to move beyond the normal range.

PROTECTING AGAINST WEAR AND TEAR

Rub the palms of your hands together rapidly. Notice how warm they get. The heat is produced by friction as the two hands rub against each other. Friction generates heat when any two surfaces rub. The rougher the surfaces are, the more heat is produced.

The ends of our bones rub against each other each time they move. If these ends were rough, our joints would get very hot, and it would hurt every time we moved. The constant friction would soon cause the ends of the bones to wear down. But this does not happen because the ends of the bones are covered with a smooth, slippery coating of cartilage. Biscuit-shaped disks of cartilage cushion the joints between the vertebrae of the spine. They act like the shock absorbers in a car. The vertebrae press on the cartilage instead of each other as we walk or run.

Each of our movable joints is surrounded by a joint capsule. These capsules contain a synovial membrane, which produces a liquid that acts as lubrication, helping to cut down on friction. Your bike has to be oiled regularly to run smoothly. So does a car or any other machine with moving parts. The lubricant in the joints of the bones is called **synovial fluid**. This lubricant is not an oil or grease. It is more like the watery saliva in your mouth or the white of an egg (*synovial* comes from the Greek word for "egg white"). Older people

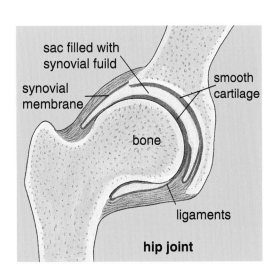

The parts of a movable joint

sac filled with synovial fuild

synovial membrane

smooth cartilage

bone

ligaments

hip joint

often do not have as much synovial fluid in their joints. That is why they may find moving difficult.

In places where tendons rub against bones, such as in the knee, small capsules or sacs can be found. These capsules, called **bursae**, contain synovial fluid to protect the tendons and bones from friction. *Bursa* is Latin for "wineskin," which was a container made out of animal skin, used to carry wine.

Have you ever heard people "crack their knuckles" or wondered about the snapping sound your knees make when you do a deep knee bend? The sound is sometimes caused by ligaments that are tightly stretched like guitar strings as they slide across a bone. Or it may be caused by bursting air bubbles in the synovial fluid in the joints. Normally there are many tiny bubbles in the fluid, but when you clench your knuckles, the bones pull apart and the bubbles join together. Then, when you "crack" the knuckles, the big bubble pops.

A gymnast must have sufficient synovial fluid in the joints to stay limber.

LOOKING AT JOINTS

Take a close look at the bone inside the plump, meaty leg of a chicken or turkey. This is the thighbone, or femur. It is long and thin, with large knobs on each end. The gristle attached to the ends of the bone is slippery cartilage, which helps to cut down on friction in the joints. The top knob is rounded. It is part of a ball-and-socket joint. What is the shape of the bone it fits into? The other end is shaped like a spool. It is part of a hinge joint. If the rest of the leg is available, see what kinds of bones fit the lower knob. Do chickens have kneecaps?

SECTION 2

SKELETAL MUSCLES

Bones cannot move without muscles. Our muscles act on our bones like the strings attached to a puppet. When a puppeteer pulls on the puppet's strings, the puppet can walk and dance. When muscles pull on our bones, we move.

Muscles make up one-third to one-half of the weight of a person's body. About 650 muscles are involved with moving parts of the body. They cover the whole skeleton. The muscles that work with the bones of the skeleton are called **skeletal muscles**.

Each skeletal muscle is attached to two parts of the body. One side is the anchor, and the other side is pulled toward the anchor. Some muscles are attached directly to two bones. But a muscle may go from a bone to the skin, or it may attach to a tendon, which is then connected to a bone. The Achilles tendon or heel cord connects a muscle in the lower leg to the heel bone.

Muscles can only pull bones; they cannot push. They contract, which means they get shorter and fatter. Bend your arm up and "make a muscle." Feel the bulge in your upper arm. This is a muscle called the biceps muscle. It is pulling on a bone in your lower arm, the radius. Now feel the calf of your leg. Stand up on your toes. The large muscle in your calf becomes even larger and firmer. This muscle is called the gastrocnemius muscle. It pulls on the heel bone.

Skeletal muscles work in pairs. If you had only a biceps muscle attached to your lower arm, once you bent it up you would not be able to straighten it out again. You would have to wait until the muscle slowly relaxed. But there is another muscle attached to the bones of the lower arm. This muscle is called the triceps muscle. It is attached to the **ulna**, the bone on the little-finger side of the lower arm. When the triceps contracts, it pulls on the ulna and straightens the arm.

Muscles help bones to support the body. Through the teamwork of muscles and bones, coordinated by messages sent through the nervous system, we are able to walk, run, jump, eat, talk, and write. Muscles and bones are working together as we throw a ball or swim. We could not even stand or sit without the support that they provide.

Every movement we make usually involves lots of different muscles. When you stand up, for example, muscles in your legs, back, shoulders, arms, and neck work together to help you rise to your feet and keep your balance—all without very much thought.

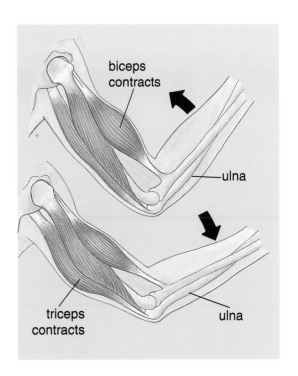

Muscles and bones work together to give the body support and movement.

MODEL OF A SKELETON

Draw the outlines of the major bones of the skeleton on a sheet of cardboard and cut them out carefully. Attach the bones together in the proper order with a needle and thread. Now you have a model of the human skeleton. Try to stand it up. It will promptly collapse. This is what would happen to a real human skeleton, standing by itself. In your body, muscles support the bones and help them to move. You can provide "muscle power" for your model skeleton by attaching strings to the skull, shoulder, arm, and leg bones. Now you can move the cardboard bones somewhat as muscles move your real bones.

HOW BONES WORK

Can you lift a 10-pound (4.5-kilogram) bag of potatoes? Probably you can, but you may find it hard work. Here's a way to make it easier: Tie a string around the top of the bag and make a loop in the free end. Lift the potatoes onto a chair. Push the end of a mop handle through the loop of string and rest the handle on the back of the chair, parallel to the floor. Now press down on the other end of the mop handle, behind the chair. It is much easier to lift the potatoes this way. You have made a model of a **lever**. This is a simple machine that helps to increase the force you can exert.

Your arm and leg bones and other long bones in your body work as levers. They are like the mop handle lever you used to increase your strength in lifting the potatoes. Muscles supply the force that moves the bones of the body.

There are three parts to a lever. Force moves the lever. The load is the object to be moved, and the lever swings or pivots at an anchor called the **fulcrum**.

There are three major types of levers. A first-class lever is the kind in a pair of scissors or a seesaw, where the fulcrum is between the force and the load. In your body, nodding your head uses the action of a first-class lever. Muscles in the back of your neck connect the back of your skull to the upper vertebrae. When these muscles contract, your head tips backward.

A second-class lever has the load between the force and the fulcrum, as in a nutcracker. You use second-class levers when you stand on tiptoe. The weight of your body rests on the balls of your feet as the calf muscles shorten, forcing your legs and body up.

A third-class lever operates in a crane, in which the force is between the load and the fulcrum. A strong cable pulls on the lifting arm to raise it. You use third-class levers to lift your arms.

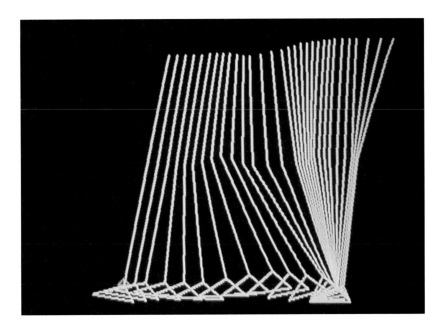

A computer-generated image of walking

WALKING IS TRICKY

Different forces and loads are involved in pushing off against the floor, swinging the other leg up, bending the knee, and all the other separate actions involved in something you do without even thinking about it.

CONTROLLING MOVEMENT

Skeletal muscles are voluntary muscles. We can control them at will. Other muscles, such as the muscles in the heart and the intestines, are involuntary muscles that work automatically.

After we are born we gradually learn to use our skeletal muscles to move various parts of the body. A baby learns to lift its head and eventually how to hold a cup, crawl, and walk. As we grow we learn how to tie our shoes and do complicated things like painting a portrait, playing the piano, or dancing.

Babies learn coordinated movements such as crawling as they become better and better at controlling skeletal muscles.

When we are learning how to do something we have to concentrate very hard at first, as the brain organizes which bones and muscles to use and in what order. Then we practice the same movements over and over so that we eventually don't have to think about what we're doing at all.

The brain works closely with the muscles and skeleton to allow us to move. Together they are called the neuromusculoskeletal system. But how does your brain tell the muscles what to do?

The brain sends messages to the body through nerves. Thin nerve fibers, like tiny threads, begin in the brain and run down the spine. From there they branch out to every part of the body. The ends of nerve cells, or neurons, touch the muscles in the body. When the brain sends electrical signals along the nerve fibers to the muscles, chemicals carry the messages to the muscle cells and cause the muscle fibers to tighten, or contract. The messages tell the muscles when, how much, and how long to contract.

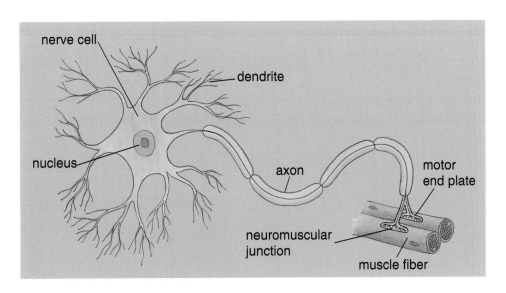

Messages from the brain to the muscles travel along nerve cells.

When each movement is completed, our sense organs send messages along other nerves, back to the brain, telling it how well we did and whether another message needs to be sent to move again. The neuro-musculoskeletal system is amazingly organized and helps us to perform complicated tasks. Even simple tasks require a lot of coordinating. Just walking uses more than a hundred muscles!

FUNCTIONS OF THE SKELETAL SYSTEM

Support and protection—these are the functions that most people think of when the bones are mentioned. The skeleton supports the body, gives it shape, and allows it to move. And it protects the delicate internal organs. The skull protects the brain, the control center for the body. The spinal cord is nearly as important as the brain, delivering messages between the body and the brain, and even controlling some parts of the body without involving the brain at all. It is protected by the backbone, or spinal column. The ribs form a bony cage that shelters the heart and lungs. The pelvis, or hipbones, helps to protect the organs in the lower part of the body. And safely sheltered inside hollows of the bones themselves is the bone marrow, the soft tissue where the blood cells are produced.

But the skeleton has another job that is just as important as protection and support. It serves as a storehouse for calcium and phosphorus. Ninety-nine percent of all the calcium in the body, for example, is stored in the bones! The other 1 percent is found in the blood and body fluids. These two minerals are very important in the workings of the body.

Calcium is needed by the nerves that stimulate muscle contractions. It is also needed for the blood to clot properly. Without it we could bleed to death. There must be a certain amount of calcium in the blood and body fluids at all times. Otherwise the muscles would contract suddenly and violently. If the calcium level of the blood drops drastically, calcium is removed from the bones.

Phosphorus is a key part of the nucleic acids, DNA and RNA. These chemicals carry the blueprints for life, the hereditary information that determines how we are formed and controls nearly every chemical reaction that goes on in the body.

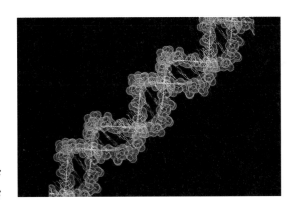

*A computer-generated image
of the DNA double helix*

We tend to think of bones as nonliving, unchanging structures, like a stone. But this is not really so. Chemicals are constantly being added to and taken away from your bones and teeth. If too much calcium is taken out of the bones, they become soft and pliable. Then the weight of the body and the pull of the muscles may push some of the long bones out of shape.

Pregnant women have to be careful to drink milk or eat cheeses and other foods rich in calcium. A growing fetus needs plenty of calcium and phosphorus to build its bones. If a pregnant woman does not take in enough of these minerals with the foods she eats, they are taken out of her own bones and teeth to supply the baby's needs.

BONE MARROW

The bone marrow is an important part of the circulatory system. It is here that the blood cells—both red cells and white cells—are made. The red cells are formed in the reddish masses of tissue known as red bone marrow. Many of the white blood cells of the body are also produced here. The next time you eat a lamb chop with a round bone, look carefully at it. Feel the soft, spongy material inside the hole. This is bone marrow.

Before you go to sleep tonight, billions of red blood cells in your body will die. But at the same time, billions of new red cells will be formed to take their place. A grown man may have as many as 25 trillion red blood cells in his body. Each one lives about four months.

There is something rather strange about red blood cells. They are the only cells in the human body that do not have nuclei, the structures that normally control a cell's activities and contain the hereditary blueprints for making new cells. The red blood cells do not start out that way. When they are first formed in the red bone marrow, each one has a nucleus—a rather large one, in fact. The red blood cell is formed from a bone marrow cell called a **stem cell**. As a new red cell develops in the bone marrow, it passes through a series of stages. The red pigment hemoglobin is produced in the maturing cells, and gives the red bone marrow its color. Gradually the nucleus disappears entirely. At last the mature red blood cell squeezes through a tiny pore into one of the blood capillaries that run through the bones and takes its place in the bloodstream. There its hemoglobin will help it to carry oxygen from the lungs to the cells of the body and carry the cells' waste carbon dioxide back to the lungs.

The stem cells of the red bone marrow can also form white blood cells. These colorless cells are the body's disease fighters. They creep and swim along the blood and lymph vessels and roam through the tissues, capturing bacteria and other invaders. There are about 700 red cells for every white cell in the blood. Some of the white cells are formed in the red bone marrow. Others are produced in the lymph nodes and spleen.

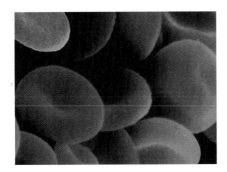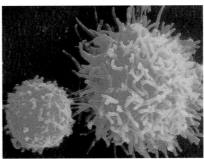

A scanning electron micrograph of human red blood cells (left) and white blood cells (right)

Red bone marrow, producing red and white blood cells, fills the hollows of most of the bones of your body. There are also some portions of yellow bone marrow, which is used to store fat and does not make blood cells. In the teen years, the marrow of the long bones of the arms and legs grows more and more fatty. By the time you are about twenty, your long bones will be filled with yellow bone marrow. Only the marrow of other bones, such as your ribs, vertebrae, and sternum (the breastbone), will still be producing red and white blood cells.

If you lose a lot of blood, from a wound or in an operation, there will not be enough red blood cells left to carry all the oxygen the body cells need. Then chemical signals in the blood will prompt the bone marrow to step up its blood cell production. Stem cells mature more quickly and in larger numbers than usual. Some regions of yellow bone marrow may even turn red and begin producing blood cells again until the emergency is over.

THE SKULL

Bones are so hard that you can feel many of them clearly through your skin. When you feel your head, it seems as though there is a bony helmet under your scalp. This is your skull. It feels like a seamless "hard hat," but actually the skull is made up of 29 bones. It starts out as individual bones, which join together as a baby grows.

The bowl-shaped top part of the skull is called the **cranium**. It protects the brain. The cranium is made of eight smooth bones that fit together tightly. The bones that make up the cranium are curved and thin. When a baby is first born there are gaps called fontanels in six places between an infant's cranial bones. In these gaps the brain is covered by a tough membrane rather than bone.

Having fontanels allows the cranium to be squeezed slightly as the baby passes through the narrow birth canal. The gaps remain during the baby's early months because the brain grows quickly. A baby's brain triples in size during the first few years. By the time a baby is two years old, its brain is nearly as large as it will be in an adult. By fifteen months to two years of age, fibrous, zigzagging joints called sutures will have tightly closed the gaps between the bones.

In the front of the skull there are 14 bones that form the shape of the face. Feel carefully around your eyes. There are round openings in the face bones here—hollow eye sockets into which the eyeballs fit.

Most of the nose that we see is made from flexible cartilage, not bone. In a skull there is a hole where the nose goes. This hole leads into the nasal cavity.

Spread your hands over your face and open your mouth wide. Which bone moved? It was the lower jawbone, called the **mandible**. Trace its outline with your fingers. The mandible is the largest, strongest bone of the face. Only the lower jawbone moves when you open and close your mouth.

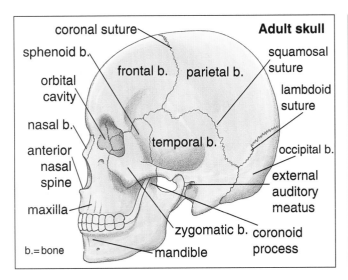

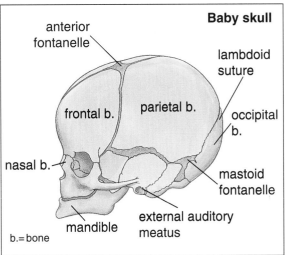

There are gaps between the bones of a baby's skull (right) to allow for a growing brain. The gaps close by about two years of age and the bones fuse. An adult skull is shown at left.

Muscles that are attached at the cheekbones and sides of the skull move the lower jaw.

The upper jaw is formed from two large **maxillary** bones that are joined together. These bones form much of the face, as well as the roof of the mouth, called the **hard palate**. Your tongue touches the hard palate when you talk, helping you to form sounds. Roots in the jawbones hold your teeth in place.

Blood vessels pass through holes in the bottom of the skull, delivering supplies of oxygen and glucose from the heart to the brain cells and carrying away their waste products. There are also openings for nerves, which link the brain with the rest of the body.

Have you ever noticed that babies' heads seem big for their size? The skull makes up one-quarter of the skeleton's length at birth, but it is only one-eighth the length of the body by the time we reach maturity.

MORE BONES THAT DON'T COUNT

Remember the sesamoid bones that don't count in the adult total of 206? Adults also have varying numbers of small bones fitted into the cranial sutures, helping to fill in the space of the fontanels. These little bones are called **wormian bones**. They were named after Olaus Worm, the Danish scientist who discovered them, not for their shape.

TEETH

The bones of the skeleton are normally covered by layers of flesh. But you also have another set of "bones" that you see every day in the mirror. These are your teeth. A person gets two sets of teeth in a lifetime. "Milk teeth" begin to form, deep inside the gums, even before a baby is born. The first ones appear at around seven months. After that a child gets about one tooth per month until the full set of 20 baby teeth have erupted.

Humans eat a very varied diet, and our teeth show it. There are several different kinds. A child has eight chisel-shaped incisors for cutting food, four pointed canines for tearing food, and eight broad molars for crushing and grinding food. Although a two-year-old child's brain is nearly adult-sized, a lot more growth will occur in the front and lower parts of the skull. As the face grows, there is room for more teeth, and larger ones. But teeth don't grow after they have erupted from the gums. Instead, the growing child gradually gets a replacement set.

At about six years of age the first permanent teeth start to appear. The jaws have grown enough so that another four molars fit in nicely behind the baby teeth. But in front, the emerging adult teeth push the baby teeth out. When baby teeth fall out you don't see any roots. As an adult tooth grows, a chemical dissolves the baby tooth's roots. The baby tooth becomes loose because it isn't rooted into a socket in the jawbone anymore.

By the age of twelve or so, the baby teeth have all been replaced by adult teeth: eight incisors, four canines, and eight premolars or bicuspids. The bicuspid—"two-pointed"—teeth are a sort of compromise in shape between canines and molars. Another four molars have been added in back, too. Sometime during the teens or early twenties, a third pair of molars—the "wisdom teeth"—appear, to complete the adult set of 32 teeth. Some people do not have enough space in their jaws for wisdom teeth, which may have to be removed.

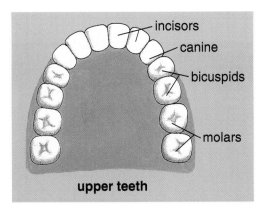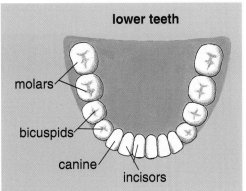

An individual usually has the above arrangement of 28 teeth by about age twelve. Sometime later, four more molars, called wisdom teeth, will come in.

Like an iceberg, most of a tooth is hidden under the surface. The part under the gum, the root, is as much as three times as long as the part that sticks out (the crown). The root is attached to the jaw by a hard, fibrous membrane, which anchors and cushions the tooth. The root is also surrounded by hard **cementum**, which helps to hold it in place.

Dentin is a bonelike substance that makes up most of the teeth. Like bone, it is 30 percent collagen and 70 percent calcium minerals and has a rich supply of blood vessels and nerves. A thick layer of **enamel** covers the crown. Enamel is the hardest substance in the body and is made up of 96 percent calcium carbonate and calcium phosphate. Enamel protects the dentin from wearing down during chewing.

Ideally our teeth should be evenly spaced, and the upper and lower rows of teeth should be arranged so that when the molars are together the upper incisors project slightly over the lower ones. However, the genes that determine the size of the teeth are inherited separately from the ones that determine the size of the jaws. Some people inherit teeth and jaws that don't go together. They may have an "overbite" in which the upper teeth stick out too far over the lower teeth. The teeth may be crowded because they are too big for the jaws. Or there may be gaps between teeth if the jaw is too big for the teeth. Such problems can be corrected using many different **orthodontic** procedures, such as braces.

THE SPINE

Bend forward and feel along the middle of your back. Do you feel little bumps running down in a straight line beginning at your neck? They are the parts of your backbone called the **vertebrae**. How many can you count? You may have as many as 33, but an adult has only 26 vertebrae.

The vertebrae fit on top of each other to form the spine. Two small pegs of bone on each one point upward and interlock with the vertebra above. Each vertebra is round in the front and has bony spikes on the sides and back. Muscles and ligaments attach to the spikes. The spine takes a lot of strain as we move and sit and stand. Ligaments hold the spine together, and it is supported by many muscles, which allow it to move.

Below each of the vertebrae is a cushion of cartilage. These shock absorbers make up about 25 percent of the spine's entire length.

DID YOU KNOW . . .

You are a fraction of an inch shorter when you go to bed than when you get up in the morning! That is because the pounding on the cartilage pads between the vertebrae during the day's activities gradually compresses them, the way a sponge rubber cushion gets squashed when you sit on it. While you sleep the disks will recover their cushiony thickness. But as you get older, they will lose some of their ability to recover. So adults actually get a little shorter as they age.

A hole passes through each vertebra to form the **spinal canal**. The spinal cord runs downward from the bottom of the brain through the spinal canal. Protecting the spinal cord is one of the spine's most important jobs. Thirty-one pairs of nerves branch off from the spinal cord to the rest of our body to control our movements and senses.

The top seven vertebrae in the neck support the skull. They are called **cervical vertebrae**. Without them, your head would droop like a wilted flower. The first vertebra is called the atlas. (In Greek myths Atlas was a giant who held up the world on his shoulders.) The atlas is not a typical vertebra. It is basically just a bony ring. The second vertebra is called the axis. It, too, is not typical. A large, toothlike structure sticks upward into the bottom of the atlas to form a pivot. The other cervical vertebrae are more typical, but they are smaller than the vertebrae below them.

After the cervical vertebrae come 12 **thoracic vertebrae** in the chest area. They are attached to the ribs. Each thoracic vertebra is larger than the one above it.

The back muscles are supported by the next five vertebrae in the lower back, called the **lumbar vertebrae**. The lumbar vertebrae are the largest and strongest of all because they bear the weight of the entire upper body when we stand.

The next five vertebrae, in the hip area, are called the **sacrum**, and they are part of the pelvis. The sacrum is made up of five separate vertebrae in children, but by the time adulthood is reached these vertebrae have fused into a single bone.

The last four vertebrae at the end of your spine, called the **coccyx**, are the "tailbones." Our evolutionary ancestors had tails, and the coccyx is all we have left. The four vertebrae that make up the coccyx also fuse together as we get older. The fusing of the sacrum and coccyx is the reason children have 33 separate vertebrae but adults have only 26.

Has anyone ever told you to sit up straight? The vertebral column is not really straight, like a broomstick, at all. It is shaped like a long double-S curve. See if you can feel the curves of your backbone. It curves back from the neck, over the broad part of the back, then swings in to the small of the back, and out again. (You can see this more clearly if you look at someone else's back.) The curves of the vertebral column make it easier to balance in an upright position, with the least possible strain from the weights of the head and body parts. An infant's spine starts out C-shaped. It is only when children begin to hold their heads up and then to sit and stand that the S curves of the spine develop.

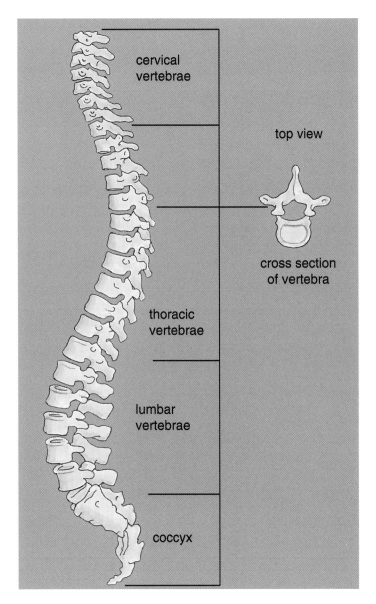

A curved spine helps us to maintain balance.

The double-S-shaped spine is springlike and flexible to allow us to twist and bend. Each joint between vertebrae can move only very slightly, but together they allow you to bend or twist your whole spine. The spine also absorbs enormous amounts of pressure when we lift, push, jump, and run. The spring shape of the spine and the cushiony cartilage between each two vertebrae reduce the impact felt by the skull when you jump hard on the ground, for example.

THE RIBS

Just as the brain is enclosed in a protective helmet of bone, so the heart and lungs are also protected by a bony framework, the ribs. The heart and lungs are our life-support system. We cannot survive without them. The lungs supply oxygen for the heart to pump around the body in our blood. The cells of our body must have oxygen in order to live. The ribs also provide protection for part of the kidneys, liver, spleen, and stomach.

The skull is solid bone, but that kind of design would not work for the ribs. Your chest cavity has to be able to move and change its shape, expanding and contracting with each breath you take. The ribs form a cage of separate bones, with spaces between them. Feel along the front of your chest, and trace the outlines of your rib cage. How many ribs can you count? They come in pairs, one on each side, and there are 24 ribs (12 pairs) all together.

Each of the ribs is attached to the spine in the back. In the front of the body, the upper seven pairs of ribs are attached by strips of cartilage called **costal cartilage** to the dagger-shaped bone called the **sternum,** or breastbone. You can feel the sternum in the middle of your chest.

The next three pairs of ribs are shorter than the others and are joined to the ribs above them by cartilage. The last two pairs of ribs are called floating ribs because they are attached only to the spine.

The ribs are strong, but flexible, flat bones. The joints at the ends of the ribs are flexible too, so that if you bump your chest the joints allow the ribs to give slightly, absorbing the shock and preventing injury to the organs inside. In severe injuries, however, the ribs can break.

The bottom of the rib cage is solid, but it is not made of bone. It is the diaphragm, a sheet of muscle that curves upward like a dome. This unusual

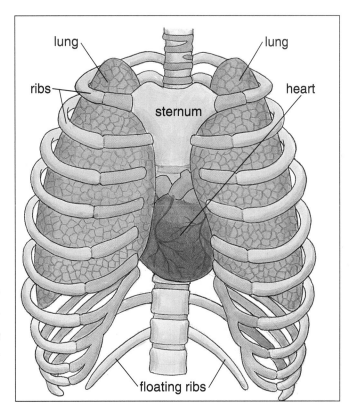

lung

lung

ribs

heart

sternum

floating ribs

The ribs provide a bony framework to protect the heart and lungs. In this drawing, part of the sternum is cut away to show the position of the heart.

muscle plays an important role in breathing. When you inhale, your diaphragm contracts and its dome shape flattens out. The chest cavity becomes larger, and so do the lungs inside it. Air rushes in through your nose and down the breathing passages into the lungs. When you exhale, your diaphragm relaxes and air is squeezed out of the lungs. Muscles between the ribs also help in breathing. When you breathe in, these muscles pull the whole rib cage upward, which enlarges the chest cavity and allows the lungs to expand. When you breathe out, the ribs fall downward and air is squeezed out of the chest.

THE SHOULDERS

If someone asked you where your shoulders are, you would probably point to the rounded "corners" just above where your arms are connected to your body. Actually, the shoulders include much more—a complex assembly of bones, muscles, and connective-tissue straps that forms the "hangers" from which the arms are suspended. Two large, flat, triangular bones called the **scapulae**, or shoulder blades, are connected to the top of the rib cage by the **clavicles**, or collarbones. The "wings" that can be seen protruding from the back of a thin person are part of the shoulder blades. The collarbones are the two curved bones that stick out on the upper part of the chest, just below the neck.

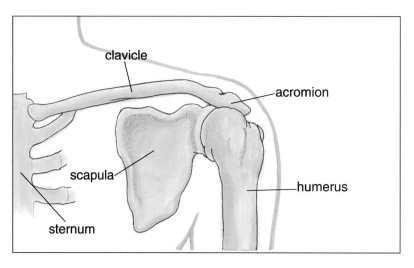

The main bones of the shoulder

A ball-and-socket joint attaches the arms to the shoulders. One end of each collarbone is connected to the breastbone. The other end is connected to the arm socket of the shoulder blade. The collarbones and shoulder blades form a sort of crossbar from which the arms hang down. This is often called the shoulder girdle. The shoulder blades are held in place by many ligaments and muscles.

Strong muscles cover the back and shoulders. These muscles allow you to move your arm. The ball-and-socket joint lets you twist, swing, and swivel your arms. The shoulder and back muscles help in lifting heavy objects. The shoulder muscles also provide support for the neck and head. The back muscles help to support the spine, so that we can stand up straight.

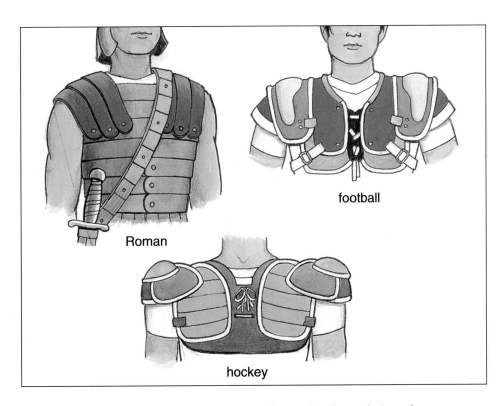

Throughout the years, special gear has been designed to protect the shoulder from injury.

THE ARMS AND HANDS

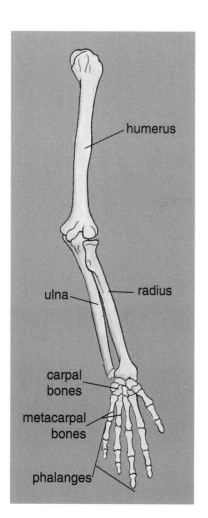

How many long bones do you have in each arm? You can feel one thick bone running the length of your upper arm. This is called the **humerus**. The upper end of the humerus is rounded like a ball. It fits into the socket of the shoulder blade. This ball-and-socket joint allows you to move your arm in a full circle.

In the forearm there are two separate, thinner long bones. When you hold your arm out with the palm up, you can feel the **radius** on the thumb side of your forearm, from the wrist to the elbow. You can feel the ulna on the other side. These bones are parallel to each other. But when you rotate your hand so that the palm is facing away from you, the two forearm bones are no longer parallel; instead, they form an X. A hinge joint at the elbow connects the two forearm bones to the humerus.

Wristwatches are really worn on the forearm, not the wrist. The wrist is made up of eight knobby **carpal bones**, situated in what people usually think of as part of the hand. The carpals are crowded together like two rows of interlocking pebbles, bound together by ligaments. Exactly how many carpals you have depends on how old you are. A baby has no carpals at all, but by the time you are grown, you will have eight carpals in each hand.

Five long bones, called **metacarpals**, form the framework of the palm of the hand. The bones of the fingers, called **phalanges**, are connected to the metacarpals. How many finger bones can you feel? There are three in each finger, but only two in the thumb. All together there are 27 bones in each hand.

The scientific name for the thumb is *pollex,* which is Latin for "strong." The pinky is *minimus,* which means "least." The ring finger is *annulary,* which means "ring." The middle finger is *medius* ("middle"), and the *index* finger gets its name from the Latin for "pointer."

Most animals walk on four legs, which is a stable design. Walking on two legs is less stable, but it allows us humans to use our hands to pick up and carry things. The human hand is amazing. It is capable of the crude force of a karate chop and of the fine skill involved in painting a portrait or performing delicate surgery on a microscopic living cell.

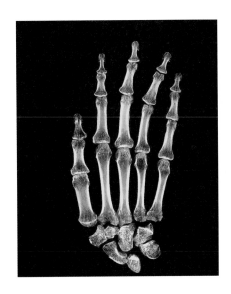

A colored X ray of the bones of a normal human hand

The many joints in our hands allow both simple and complicated movements. Three hinge joints in each finger allow us to grasp things. The thumbs have a saddle joint that permits movement in two directions. In addition, the thumbs are set lower on our hands than our other fingers, and can bend toward the fingers. This arrangement is called an opposable thumb. It allows us to hold on to things and do special tasks like threading a needle. Very few animals have opposable thumbs.

Muscles below the elbow control the movement of the lower arm and wrist. Muscles above the elbow allow us to raise and lower the arm.

Three sets of nerves come from the spinal cord, along the shoulders and down the arms. When you bump your funny bone you are pressing on a nerve that passes under the end of the humerus. *Humerus* sounds like "humorous," which means funny—that is how this body part got its name. But the tingling sensation is not a humorous experience.

THE PELVIS

Place your hands on your hips and feel the hard ridge that curves around to the lower part of your back. This is the **pelvis**. This basin-shaped structure sticks out at the sides to form what we call our hips. (*Pelvis* is the Latin word for "basin.") The pelvis is made up of several different bones, which are firmly joined together. The sacrum connects the pelvis to the spine, and the pelvis supports the bottom of the spine. The other bones that make up the pelvis are the **ilium, ischium,** and **pubis**. By the time we reach late adolescence, these three bones have fused together.

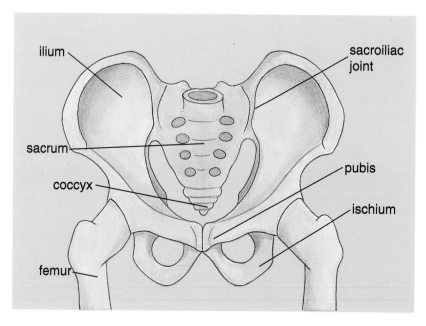

The pelvic skeleton of an adult

The ilium, ischium, and pubis join in a cup-shaped socket, into which the leg bone is attached in a ball-and-socket joint. Like the shoulders, the pelvis is called a girdle because it attaches the legs to the skeleton.

Whereas the shoulder girdle moves freely on the trunk, the pelvic girdle is fixed in place by some of the strongest and tightest ligaments in the body. The hip joints have traded some movement for greater strength and stability.

In addition to providing a place for the legs to attach, the pelvis also protects the soft organs of the abdominal cavity: the bladder, where urine is stored, and the large intestines, through which solid wastes pass to be excreted. Women have larger pelvises than men. The uterus, where a baby grows inside its mother, is protected in a woman's pelvic basin.

Muscles called the gluteus maximus (*maximus* means "biggest," and *gluteus* is Greek for "rump") are found at the back of the pelvis. They are the largest muscles in the body and help support your upper body as you walk, as well as allowing you to turn your hips. Each muscle covers a fatty pad; together they form the buttocks that we sit on.

THE LEGS AND FEET

The leg bones are very much like arm bones, but they are much bigger. The **femur**, which extends from the pelvis to the knee, is the longest, heaviest, and strongest bone in the body. It is connected to the hip in a ball-and-socket joint like the shoulder joint. A hinge joint at the knee connects the femur to two thinner bones. The **tibia**, or shinbone, is at the front of your lower leg. The even thinner **fibula** is alongside.

The knee is a hinge joint like the elbow. This joint is open when you stand up and fully closed when you squat on your knees. When you run, this hinge opens and closes. The knee is protected by a teardrop-shaped bone called the **patella**, or kneecap.

The bones that stick out at our "ankles" are the lower part of the fibula and tibia. The back of the foot, where our ankle really is, is formed by the **calcaneus** (heel bone) and six other bones called **tarsals**. Notice that the ankle has only seven bones, whereas each wrist has eight carpal bones.

In the middle of the foot are five **metatarsals**. These are connected to the toe bones, which, like the finger bones, are called phalanges. The bones of the toes are similar to those of the fingers, but they are not able to move as well, and the big toes are not opposable to the other toes as our thumbs are. Our monkey and ape relatives have opposable thumbs on their feet as well as their hands.

The little toe helps us keep our balance. When we walk we push off with our big toe. But we do not use our toes very much. Humans have the potential for far more use of their feet. Some people have learned to use their feet to feed themselves, paint pictures, use a typewriter, and even play the piano. But in most humans, feet quickly develop into specialized tools, which are not only walked on but are often abused by being jammed into tight-fitting shoes that cramp the toes, or into high heels that throw the body's weight forward onto the metatarsals, which were never designed to bear the full load of the body.

Our legs are much stronger than our arms. They have thicker, longer bones and are moved by much more powerful muscles. When you run, your legs are subjected to a force of five or more times your body weight. Jumping multiplies the force even more.

The thigh muscles raise and lower the leg. The muscles in the lower part of the leg control the movement of the ankles, feet, and toes. These muscles are joined to the heel by the Achilles tendon.

Our feet balance and support the weight of the whole body. They cushion the impact when we run or jump. We put hundreds of tons of weight on our feet each day from all the walking we do.

Thirty-three joints in each foot help to support the body and allow us to walk and run. One hundred flat, bandagelike ligaments in each foot hold all the bones, joints, and tendons in place. Skeletal muscles in the foot keep the bones of the foot in place and pull on tendons to move the foot and toes.

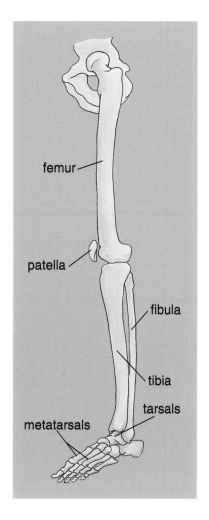

The bones of the leg and foot

We are all born with flat feet. When a child starts to walk, the muscles and ligaments in the foot become stronger and the bones of the foot rise to form an arch. An arch provides great strength for bearing weight, yet the tendons and ligaments that bind the bones together allow a certain degree of give; thus, the feet can also spring and lift for movements. By the age of sixteen, the arch is usually complete; however, those who do a lot of walking or running may remain flat-footed.

SECTION 3

YOUR SKELETON'S LIFE STORY

Three months after you were conceived, while you were still in your mother's womb, you had a complete skeleton—but there was not a single bone in your body. Instead, your skeleton was made of soft, rubbery cartilage. Little by little the cartilage was replaced by bone. Even when you were born, much of your skeleton was still cartilage. This was a good thing, for the softness of your "bones" helped you to squeeze through the birth opening more easily. Perhaps your head looked a little lopsided for the first day or two. Your skull was still so soft that it was easily molded.

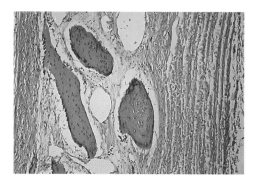

Developing bone membrane in a fetus

You grew very quickly before you were born. In nine months you went from a tiny dot no bigger than a pinpoint to a miniature human about 20 inches (51 centimeters) long. After birth you continued to grow rapidly. In your first year you probably tripled your weight, and by the end of your second year you were already about half the height you will be when you are an adult. Real bone filled in the cartilage "model" of your skeleton, and with this added support you were soon able to hold your head up, sit, stand, and walk. Your bones continued to grow, along with the rest of your body, and they are still growing. They will probably continue to grow until your middle or late teens, when you have reached your full height.

Slowly, over the years, more and more cartilage becomes bone. By the time you get to be twenty-five years old, your bones will be only 30 percent living tissue—the rest will be nonliving minerals. The cartilage in your nose and ears, however, will remain as cartilage for your whole life.

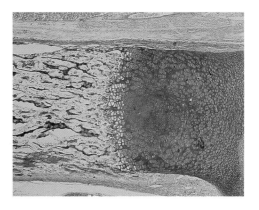

Bone (left portion of the photograph) gradually replaces the cartilage skeleton of a developing baby.

HOW BONES GROW

Bone is hard and firm. It does not stretch or bend. Much of it is made of minerals, just like a stone. How can it grow?

Part of the answer is cartilage. When bone replaced the cartilage in your baby skeleton, not all of this rubbery tissue disappeared. A cover of cartilage remained on the ends of the bones, helping to smooth the joints. And thin plates of cartilage remained where the large ends of the bone were joined to the thinner shaft or middle portion.

The end portion of a long bone is called the **epiphysis**. The shaft is called the **diaphysis**. The cartilage plate that separates these two plates is an important growth center. The cartilage cells on the side of the plate next to the epiphysis continually multiply, forming rows and columns of cartilage cells.

On the other side of the plate, bone cells and blood vessels push into the cartilage and replace it with bone. The bone-building cells that make new bone tissue are called **osteoblasts**. Their name means "bone formers." Bone cells of another kind also

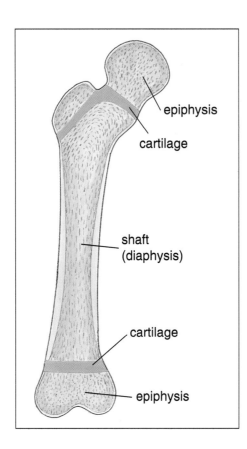

Cartilage areas at the ends of long bones are growth centers.

epiphysis

cartilage

shaft
(diaphysis)

cartilage

epiphysis

play an important part in the growth of bones. They are **osteoclasts**, or "bone breakers."

Bone breakers eat away channels in the cartilage. Bone builders follow them and coat the channels with layers of collagen. Then calcium phosphate is laid onto the intricate crisscrossing collagen fibers, and so new bone is formed and the shafts of the bones grow longer. The replacement of soft cartilage with bone is called **ossification**. It begins before birth and continues until the end of puberty.

Finally, when you have finished growing, the cartilage cells in the growth plate stop multiplying. The cartilage is replaced by bone, and the growth plate disappears. The epiphysis and diaphysis are joined together by bone. Only the ends of the bones retain a cartilage covering to prevent wear and tear.

What about the bone marrow cavities? Your bones are now much larger than they were when you were a baby. And as you continue to grow, they will get larger still. There was room for only a tiny marrow cavity in each bone when you were first born. If growth of bones meant just adding new solid bone to the ends, the marrow cavities could never get any bigger than they were when you were a baby. Yet the marrow cavities in your bones run nearly the whole length of the bones. Bone breakers eat away bone tissue from the ends of the marrow cavities, so that these hollows inside the bones keep growing as long as the bones themselves do.

BUILDING UP AND BREAKING DOWN

Even after you have reached your full height, your bones will not lose all of their ability to grow. Although bones seem to be unchanging, they are living tissues. Like the other tissues of the body, parts of the bones are constantly being built up and broken down. Normally these two processes just balance each other, and the bones seem to be unchanged. Under normal conditions as much as 10 percent of an adult skeleton is replaced each year. But under some conditions, one process—either buildup or breakdown of bone—may go faster than the other.

Even if an adult breaks a bone, the broken ends will grow together and heal the fracture. In fact, if a broken bone heals together crookedly, an X ray taken a few years later may show no signs of the mistake. Osteoblasts build up one part of the bone, while osteoclasts are eating away another, until it looks normal. In older people the bone-repair systems do not work as well, and a thickened place may remain where a broken bone has healed.

After you are fifty or so, the breakdown of bone may be slightly faster than the buildup of new bone. People tend to get a little shorter after this age, and their bones may become lighter and weaker. This thinning of the bones with age is called **osteoporosis**. The bones of very old people may break so easily that when you hear of someone who has "fallen and

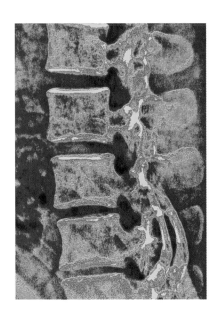

An X ray of the spine shows bone loss in the vertebrae (squares). They are thinning due to osteoporosis.

broken a hip," the reverse may really have happened—the bone was so weakened that it broke, and then the person fell down.

Bone is not just replaced, it is remodeled to adapt to pressures that are placed on it. Bones become thicker when a load is placed on them.

Your bones will get stronger and thicker if you do a lot of heavy work or exercise, even after you are an adult. A runner's leg bones or the hands of someone who does a lot of manual labor will thicken to cope with the increased demand on the bones. Horseback riders have thickened bone on their buttocks. Students develop bone bumps on their fingers where pencils press against the bones.

Bones become thinner when pressure is taken off them. Pencil bumps disappear gradually if you stop writing so much.

HOW DO BRACES GET TEETH TO MOVE?

Braces put pressure against the sockets where teeth are rooted in the jaw. Osteoclasts eat away bone at the pressure points in the socket, leaving a space for the tooth to move into. On the other side of the socket, osteoblasts fill in new bone that helps to hold the tooth in its new position. So the tooth sockets in the jawbone have actually moved.

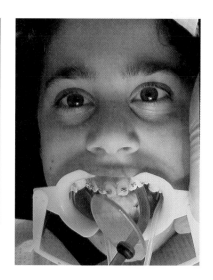

CONTROLLING GROWTH

How tall are you? How tall do you think you will be when you are fully grown? This will depend on a number of things. If your father and mother are tall, there is a good chance that you will be tall, too. For we inherit the tendency to grow tall or short just as we inherit blue or brown eyes, and brown or blond hair.

To a great extent, hormones control how much we grow and when we stop growing. One of the most important of these is human growth hormone. It is produced in the pituitary gland, a pea-sized structure just under the brain. If your pituitary gland does not make enough growth hormone, you might be a dwarf. If too much is produced, you may become a giant. Basketball players who are more than 7 feet (2.1 meters) tall probably had an unusually high amount of growth hormone in their blood in their growing years. Most people's pituitary glands produce just enough human growth hormone so that they can grow to a height between 5 and 6 feet (1.5 and 1.8 meters).

The food we eat also helps to determine how tall we will grow. Eating enough protein is especially important during the growing years because proteins are one of the basic building blocks for new tissues. Vitamins and minerals are important, too. As you grow taller, your bones are growing larger. You must have new supplies of calcium and phosphorus each day to build strong bones. You can get them by drinking milk and eating cheeses.

Even if you are getting enough of these minerals in your foods, your body will not be able to use them properly unless you also have enough of certain vitamins, especially vitamin D. This vitamin helps the body to absorb calcium and phosphorus from food in the intestines. It is formed by cells in the skin when it is exposed to the sun. Children who do not get enough vitamin D may develop **rickets**. They become "bowlegged" or "knock-kneed" because the growing bones did not get enough minerals, and they become so soft that they are bent out of shape by the body's weight. The sternum may also be distorted, producing a protruding pigeon breast. Rickets can be cured by taking extra doses of vitamin D, with a diet that has plenty of calcium and phosphorus. Your grandparents probably had to take a dose of cod liver oil each day to get enough vitamin D (fish oils are rich in vitamin D). Now vitamin D is added to milk, so that you get all the important bone builders at the same time.

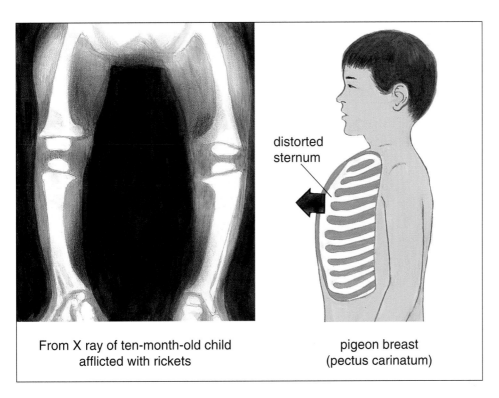

From X ray of ten-month-old child afflicted with rickets

distorted sternum

pigeon breast (pectus carinatum)

Children who do not get enough vitamin D may develop bowlegs (left) and pigeon breast (right), signs of rickets.

EXERCISE AND BONE GROWTH

The amount your bones will grow also depends to some degree on how much exercise you get. The more stress that is put on a bone, the more it will grow. One scientist took two groups of baby rats and fed hard food to one group and soft food to the other. Both diets had the same amount of nourishment. But the rats that had to chew more developed slightly larger heads and faces, and their head and jaw bones were quite a bit heavier.

An astronaut exercises on a treadmill to help maintain strong bones while in space.

Athletes usually develop much stronger and heavier bones than people who do not get much exercise. But if you were kept in bed for a long time, your bones would become thinner and weaker. When no stress is put on bones, calcium salts are carried away by the blood, and the bones themselves actually become smaller. When you got up again, you might be in some danger of breaking your bones, until they had a chance to grow strong again. This kind of bone thinning can be a real problem for hospital patients, and it is also a concern for astronauts who go on long space missions under weightless or low-gravity conditions.

Without the pull of gravity, minerals are dissolved out of the bones and lost from the body. When astronauts go on long flights or stay in orbit for long periods, during which there is little or no gravity pulling on them, their bones become weak, and the fine balance of minerals in their blood may be upset. Astronauts on early space missions were found to lose 0.14 ounce (4 grams) of calcium per month spent in space. Special exercise plans while astronauts are in space help to keep their bodies in good condition and keep their bones from wasting away.

GROWTH RATES AND SEX DIFFERENCES

Have someone measure the lengths of your head, trunk, arms, and legs and draw them to scale on a piece of paper. Compare these with the measurements of your parents and a baby. Figure out what fraction each body part is compared to the total height of the figure.

You may be surprised to find that a baby's head is nearly as large as yours, and your head is nearly as large as your parents'. Yet you are much taller than a baby, and your parents are still taller than you. How could the proportions change so much?

The bones of the body do not all grow at the same rate. The skull grows rather slowly, while the long bones grow more rapidly. The bones of the arms and legs grow faster than the bones of the trunk. Gradually the proportions of the body change, and the length of the head takes a much smaller fraction of the whole length of the body than it did at birth.

During your growing years, you do not always grow at the same rate. Did your parents keep a height record for you? If you examine the record you will see that in some years you added barely an inch to your height, while in other years you may have grown three or four inches or even more.

A big "growth spurt" comes during adolescence, when your body is changing from a child into an adult. During that time sex hormones work with growth hormones to help your body grow. These sex hormones are responsible for the differences between the skeleton of a man and that of a woman.

The male sex hormones, called androgens, help the bones to grow strong and thick. They cause the shoulder bones to grow broader. Female sex hormones, the estrogens, tend to make the hipbones broader. In a woman, the space between the hipbones, the pelvic cavity, is wider than it is in a man's body. A child's trunk is shaped like a rectangle. But the trunk of a fully grown male looks more like a triangle standing on its point. A woman's trunk looks more like a triangle standing on its base.

Before puberty, the stage of growth in which the sex organs mature, boys and girls are usually about the same height. But most men are taller than most women. The reason is that puberty usually comes later in boys than in girls. Before puberty, the legs grow faster than the trunk, but after the sexual development is complete, the growth of the long bones soon stops. So boys have a year or two more "growing time."

BROKEN BONES, STRAINS, AND SPRAINS

Our skeletons are well suited to stand up to the pressures and strains that normal everyday living places upon them. However, sometimes things go wrong.

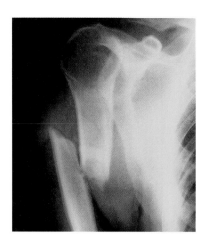

This X ray of a broken upper arm bone shows a severe compound fracture.

Broken bones are one of the most dramatic skeletal injuries. A broken bone is called a **fracture**. In a simple fracture, the bone breaks but does not stick out through the skin. A broken bone is called a compound fracture (or open fracture) if the bone pierces the skin.

Injuries to joints in the legs—especially the knees—are the most common sports injuries. Strains, sprains, and dislocations are the most frequent injuries.

A **dislocation** occurs when a bone slips out of its joint. Ligaments and tendons can be torn or overstretched when a bone becomes dislocated; or a nerve may be pinched, causing a lot of pain. A **slipped disk** is a special kind of dislocation, in which the pads of cartilage between the vertebrae in the spine slip out of place and press on the spinal cord. When a slipped disk presses on the sciatic nerve, which passes through the spine, it can cause **sciatica**—a sharp pain that runs from the buttock down one leg to the toes.

When the upper arm slips out of the shoulder socket, a doctor can often easily put it back into place, but it may hurt for a while. The doctor may advise a person with a dislocated shoulder to wear an arm sling for up to a month while the ligaments heal and shorten to their normal length.

Strains occur when tendons or muscles such as those in the lower back are twisted or overstretched. In **tennis elbow** the tendons on the outside of the elbow joint become inflamed. Tennis elbow can develop from other activities besides tennis. When you hold your arm out with the palm upward, the radius and ulna run side by side. But when you rotate your forearm so that the palm faces down, the radius lies across the ulna. The muscles can become strained if you overdo this kind of twisting motion.

When ligaments that hold a joint together are overstretched, the injury is called a **sprain**. Pain and swelling may occur. A sprained ankle may get better if you elevate your foot and wrap your ankle with cold bandages. Stretching or other warm-up exercises before the muscles have to do hard work can help prevent many sport injuries.

Backaches are among the commonest skeletal system complaints. It has been estimated that three out of four people suffer from back pain from time to time. Some backaches are due to old age or defects that people are born with, but most are the result of weakened back muscles due to lack of exercise or stress. Lower back pain is one of the most frequent problems. Back muscle or ligament strain can cause a pain in the lower back called **lumbago**.

People who are overweight and those who have jobs that are partly active and partly sedentary, such as truck drivers, need to be especially careful not to put too much strain on the back. One important key is to practice proper lifting by bending the knees so that the legs can bear some of the burden.

HOW BROKEN BONES HEAL

A large blood clot forms and starts to harden around the broken ends of the bone. Bone-forming osteoblasts move from the outer layers of the bone into the gap between the broken ends. These cells form a bridge of collagen fibers between the broken ends of the bone. The ends of the bone become soft as minerals seep out and calcium salts are deposited in the matrix. New bone is growing. This new growth joining the broken ends is called a **callus**. Gradually, the callus starts to harden to form true bone. When it is completely hardened, the bone is as strong as though it had never been broken. The technique of applying a small electrical charge to the break is often used to speed up healing. Not only do broken bones heal in half the time with electric current, but there is much less damage to the muscles attached to the bones.

PAINFUL BONES AND JOINTS

When the calcium level in the body drops, this mineral is taken out of the bones. Exercise helps the body to work more efficiently and makes bones sturdier. Lack of exercise and a lack of calcium-rich foods in the diet, plus a decrease in vitamin D from lack of exposure to the sun, can result in brittle bones that may break easily, a condition known as osteoporosis. It is most common in older women. After menopause, a decrease in the estrogen hormones also contributes to osteoporosis.

When a person has **rheumatoid arthritis**, joints become swollen and painful. Rheumatoid arthritis begins when the synovial membranes become inflamed, producing heat, swelling, and pain in the joints. The inflammation may spread, causing the cartilage on the ends of the bones to thin and disappear. The ligaments and tendons may also become inflamed, causing even more pain and stiffness. Doctors believe that the body's own defense system attacks the joint tissues, mistaking them for invading germs.

Too much wear and tear on joints can cause **osteoarthritis**. Bony joints and gnarled hands are common in elderly people who have done manual labor all their lives. What happens is that the cartilage in the joints wears down. Without this protective pad, the bones in the joint rub against each

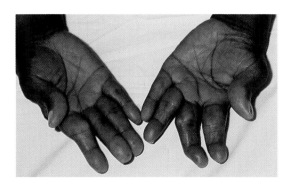

Rheumatoid arthritis can cause pain and deformity. It is an autoimmune disorder in which the immune system acts against the body's joints.

other. This irritates the periosteum, the protective membrane around the bones, and the bones thicken at the areas of irritation. Osteoarthritis occurs most often in the finger, hip, spine, and knee joints. Recently, a new technique to regenerate damaged cartilage offers hope to many people who have cartilage problems. Healthy cartilage cells are taken from a patient and are grown and multiplied in the lab for two weeks, then injected into the patient's damaged joint, relieving pain.

Bursitis is an inflammation of the fluid-filled sacs (bursae) in the joints, usually as a result of repeated pressure. The joints become swollen and painful. People who kneel to scrub floors or lay carpets may develop bursitis in the knees ("housemaid's knee"). Leaning on your elbow while reading or studying may produce a painful swelling in the bursa at the tip of the elbow ("student's elbow"). Rest, ice packs, and drugs to reduce inflammation usually help the joint to absorb the excess fluid and return to normal.

In modern factories and offices, some workers are developing various repetitive motion injuries. When a person performs the same action over and over, especially on machines that are not well designed to work with human body structures, the kind of wear and tear that could lead to osteoarthritis over a long lifetime is greatly speeded up. Typists, for example, may develop a condition called **carpal tunnel syndrome**. The tendons running through narrow channels in the wrist bones become inflamed and press on the nerves that pass into the hand. Pain and stiffness of the hands and numbness of the fingers may result. Playing video games too long without a break can also lead to repetitive motion injuries.

In a disease called **gout**, the body does not properly dispose of a waste product called uric acid. Crystals form in some joints, especially in the big toe, making them swollen and painful.

Some people suffer from **TMJ** (**temporomandibular joint disorder**). Their jaws may ache, and there is a clicking sound and pain when they open their mouths. There may be ringing in the ears and frequent headaches. Many things can cause TMJ. Some people clench their jaws or grind their teeth when they feel stress, during the day or even while they sleep. TMJ can also be caused by misaligned jaws or teeth. Opening and closing the mouth is controlled by five muscles. Overtensing the muscles can put pressure on the temporomandibular joint where the jaw connects to the skull. The clicking sound occurs when the bone slips over cartilage.

SKELETAL DEFORMITIES

Many types of skeletal deformities are caused by errors that occur while a fetus is developing inside its mother. Certain bones may fail to form in the developing fetus, or may be formed abnormally. Such conditions as **cleft palate** and **spina bifida** are the result of failure of bones to fuse on schedule.

The roof of the mouth is formed by the two large bones (maxillae) that make up the upper jaw and a large part of the facial structure. The two maxillae are joined along the midline. If a part of these bones does not join properly during prenatal development, a cleft palate results.

Spina bifida develops when the bones of the spine do not fuse properly and a portion of the spinal cord may stick out through the opening of the bone.

Talipes or clubfoot is a malformation in which the foot is twisted out of shape or position. It may be due to a genetic disorder in the child or a disease suffered or drug taken by the mother during pregnancy.

Injury, disease, or poor posture may distort the normal spine curvature. Quasimodo, the Hunchback of Notre Dame, is the most famous sufferer of **kyphosis**, an abnormal bulging of the upper part of the spine. In kyphosis the normal backward curve of the upper part of the spine is greatly exaggerated. This condition can cause lung and heart problems because it decreases the amount of space for the organs inside the body. An exaggerated lumbar curvature is known as **lordosis**, or swayback. Perhaps you have been checked in school for **scoliosis**. This is a sideways curvature of the spine, involving rotation of the vertebrae. Scoliosis may develop during childhood or adolescence. It may be caused by malformation of some of the vertebrae or a muscle problem that results in an uneven pull on the spine. The curvature shows up very clearly on X rays, but it can also be detected by a simple screening test: when a person with scoliosis bends over, the back is higher on one side instead of forming a smoothly rounded curve. Wearing a brace or a series of casts while the spine is finishing its growth may help to bring an abnormal curve back to normal. Sometimes a spinal fusion operation is used to treat scoliosis. The cartilage between some of the vertebrae is removed, and they grow together into a solid column of bone, which holds the spine straighter.

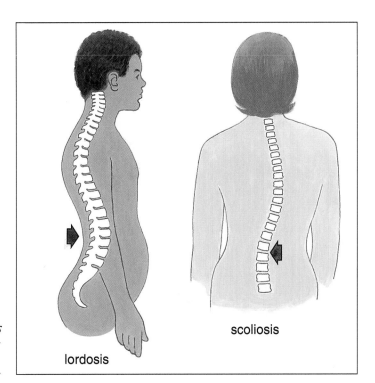

Lordosis (left) and scoliosis (right) are abnormal curvatures of the spine.

lordosis

scoliosis

In **acromegaly**, the bones of the face, hands, and feet are enlarged. This condition is caused by the secretion of too much growth hormone after the growth of the long bones has ended.

A **bunion** is a bulging of the joint at the base of the big toe. Bunions tend to run in families. Women have bunions three times as often as men. The joint at the base of the big toe normally bulges a little. Tight-fitting shoes can press on the joint, causing inflammation and a thickening of the bone there. Corns or infections may develop, too. The big toe may press on other toes and become distorted. Proper-fitting shoes are important for everyone, especially those with bunions.

TREATING SKELETAL PROBLEMS

If you've ever had a broken arm, your arm swelled up and hurt terribly. At first the doctor may not have been sure whether the bone was broken or just badly bruised. An X-ray picture was taken to make sure. X rays are radiations, just as light rays are. We cannot see X rays, but they show up on photographic film. They can pass easily through the soft tissues of the body, but bone stops them, so in an X-ray picture the doctor can see exactly where the break is. With the X-ray picture as a guide, the doctor can set the fracture by moving the arm until the broken ends of the bone are neatly fitted together.

For a fracture to heal properly, the broken parts of the bone must be held perfectly still. If they are allowed to move, they may come apart again, or the ends of the bone may grow together crookedly. That is why a doctor places a broken arm or other broken bone in a snug cast, a casing of plaster or fiberglass to prevent the arm from moving.

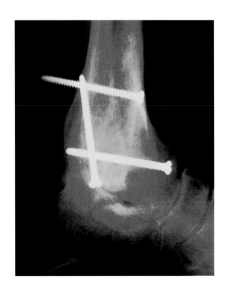

This badly broken ankle needed screws to hold the bones in place until they healed.

When some bones, such as the femur in the leg, are broken, a simple cast may not be enough to help the bone heal. The muscles attached to the femur are very strong and could pull the bone apart inside the cast. The patient may have to be in **traction**. A weight pulls against the muscles to prevent them from pulling the bone apart.

If a bone is badly broken or smashed, a special doctor called an **orthopedic surgeon** may have to screw or pin pieces of bone together. Orthopedic specialists may also be consulted to treat other skeletal system problems. Corrective casts and braces may be used to straighten abnormal curvatures of the spine. Surgery can help to correct skeletal problems that developed when bones did not form properly, such as cleft palate or talipes. Diseases that damage or destroy the bone marrow may be treated with a bone marrow transplant. Bone marrow drawn out of the bones of another person replaces the unhealthy bone marrow and begins making new blood cells.

Doctors have many sophisticated tools to diagnose skeletal problems. Scanners that build up an image by bouncing ultrasound waves off internal body structures may be used to determine whether a baby's hip joints have formed properly. Dislocation of the hips is a fairly common congenital problem—one that developed before birth. Fortunately, when it is detected early, it is easily fixed with braces or casts. Sometimes just using a double diaper, which holds the baby's legs out at right angles, is enough to mold the still-forming bones into a better fit.

A sports star with a knee injury may be checked by arthrography. A dye is injected into the knee, and damaged cartilage in the joint will show up on an X ray. Or the orthopedic surgeon may use an **arthroscope** to find the problem and fix it in one operation. This handy tool is a thin tube containing light-transmitting glass fibers, which can light up the interior of the joint and transmit a picture of it back to the surgeon. The arthroscope is also equipped with tiny tools that the surgeon can use to remove misplaced bone growths or repair torn cartilage and ligaments. Only a small incision is needed—just enough to slip in the arthroscope—and the whole procedure can be done in an outpatient facility.

Physical therapists are an important part of the medical team treating people with skeletal system problems. After an injury, a healed joint or limb may be weak and stiff. Physical therapy, including heat or ice treatments, massage, and carefully supervised exercises, can help to restore strength and motion. Physical therapists also help people with arthritis to regain mobility in the damaged joints, and they aid people who have been sick in bed for a long time to rebuild their wasted bones and muscles.

People suffering from backaches that won't go away may go to a **chiropractor**. *Chiro-* comes from a word for "hand." Chiropractors use their hands to move or manipulate parts of the spine in hopes of removing pressure on the nerves. Another type of doctor called an **osteopath** uses manipulation and massage to help with bone-related aches and pains.

ARTIFICIAL LIMBS

Artificial limbs have been used for hundreds of years to replace the limb of a person who has lost an arm or a leg. In the past, artificial limbs were heavy and clumsy, with stiff joints (if they had any joints at all). Today's artificial limbs not only look much more realistic but move very much like a real limb. They may be made of plastic, metal, wood, or leather.

An artificial leg has a hip joint, knee joint, and ankle joint just like a real leg, but the artificial leg weighs only half of what a real leg weighs. It is attached to the body by straps. It may take a person many months to learn

This woman's artificial right leg looks very realistic. While wearing it, she can enjoy a number of sports.

how to use an artificial limb. Muscles in the upper part of the body swing the artificial leg forward.

Researchers are working on replacement arms and legs that are even closer to their real-life models. One type contains tiny motors controlled by a computer chip programmed to open and close a hand and produce other lifelike movements. In "bionic" limbs, movements are powered by tiny electrical impulses from the nerves in the stump. So the wearer of a bionic arm could produce movements of the hand by thinking, in the same way that the brain controls a natural arm.

KEEPING THE SKELETON HEALTHY

Medicine has made great advances in diagnosing and treating various skeletal problems. But it is generally a lot easier to prevent problems than to cure them.

An important part of preventive care for your skeleton is good posture. When you stand, your spine should be gently curved, with the head and shoulders comfortably balanced and the weight of the body evenly resting on both feet. When you slouch or slump—whether sitting or standing—your muscles sag. If you let your shoulders slump forward, the pelvis and stomach go forward, too, and the back muscles tighten. Bad posture can cause tiredness and chronic back strain.

But bad posture is a habit that we can control. Sitting and standing straight, sleeping in a bed that supports the back, and bending the knees when you lift heavy objects can help to avoid back problems.

Some sensible precautions can also do a lot to prevent repetitive motion injuries and other problems that develop at work and play. A new science called **ergonomics** aims at designing tools and furniture that are comfortable, easy to operate, and generally user-friendly. Well-designed computer desks, for example, can help to reduce aches and pains by putting the monitor at a level where it is easy to look at without straining and by providing support for the wrists while typing. But some other preventive measures are just good common sense. To avoid bursitis in your knees, wear cushiony knee pads when you work in the garden or do something else that requires a lot of kneeling. And repetitive motion injuries won't develop if you take frequent rest or exercise breaks. You may get so absorbed in a video game or computer program that it seems hard to tear yourself away, but you'll feel better if you do.

Stretching exercises help keep muscles and joints from getting stiff. Moderate exercise is often helpful in keeping muscles and bones healthy. That's a preventive lesson many of us need to learn. Most people today are less active than our ancestors were. Many adults sit at a desk job all day, drive to and from work, and then sit down in front of the television at night. Even children spend less time in physical activities than the children of past generations.

In addition, most people do not eat very wisely. We eat a lot of junk foods that may not have all the vitamins and minerals we need. As we have seen, minerals like calcium and phosphorus and vitamin D are important for healthy bones. But many adults do not drink milk or eat dairy products, important sources of these nutrients.

Exercise and eating well are important for keeping our skeletal systems healthy.

Exercise helps to keep the body healthy.

CLUES TO THE PAST

When a human skeleton is dug up and the police suspect that a murder may have been committed, a **forensic scientist** is called to the scene. After studying the bones, the expert can tell whether the victim was a man or woman, his or her age at the time of death, and when the death occurred. The expert may be able to tell what caused the death, and can reconstruct the person's general appearance—height, weight, and even facial features—with startling accuracy. With this information, the detectives have a good start on their investigation of the crime.

Bones can help in solving much older mysteries, too. The bones of animals that lived thousands and even millions of years ago hold important clues to the history of life on earth.

READING THE BONES

If you found a skeleton in your closet, you could figure out whether it belonged to a male or a female. The biggest clue is the pelvis. A woman's pelvis is wider than a man's and has a large opening. The opening in a man's pelvis is smaller and heart-shaped. In addition, a man's bones are usually larger and heavier. A woman's breastbone is wider and shorter. Her wrists and jaw bones are smaller. A male's eyebrow ridges are thicker.

Vitruvius, an ancient Roman architect, devised a way to tell how tall a person was by measuring the bones in the arms. A person's height can be calculated by multiplying the length of the hand by ten. Our height is also equal to the distance between our fingertips when we hold our arms all the way out to the sides. Other, more accurate formulas have been devised, but these simple rules are usually pretty good approximations.

Bones are the hardest parts of the body. When an old cemetery is dug up, bare skeletons are found in the graves. The soft flesh on the bodies that were buried there has decayed, and even the wood of the coffins may be gone, but the bones still seem unchanged. Yet if enough years go by, the minerals can be washed out of the bones by the water and acids in the soil, and the bones themselves may disappear. How, then, do **paleontologists** (scientists who study the remains of ancient creatures) have anything left to study?

The remains of ancient creatures, called **fossils**, can be preserved in various ways. In some caves, particularly in desert regions where the air is very dry, the bodies of animals may be covered over with soil or rocks that have fallen from the roof of the cave. In these sheltered places the bones may remain undisturbed until someone happens to dig in the cave. Sometimes animals are trapped in quicksand, in great pits of sticky tar, under rockfalls or flows of hot lava from volcanoes, or in the moving ice of glaciers. Their bones, or even whole bodies, may be preserved there.

As the years go by, dust and soil are blown about and carried by flooding rivers. A new layer of soil builds up over the bodies of the buried animals, and new plants begin to grow. They in turn die and are covered by new layers of soil. Many years go by—hundreds, thousands, millions of years. The buried layers of soil turn into rock. Bones and shells and other hard parts of animals' bodies may be preserved in these rocks.

Waters flowing underground may dissolve parts of these remains, leaving spaces in the rocks like the hollows in a mold. This is a very slow process, and the softest parts dissolve first. After a hollow is formed, minerals may be deposited in it, filling the hollow just as you fill a mold with plaster of paris. Slowly a rock model or cast is formed, which is a nearly perfect copy of the original form. If it was a bone, for example, the rock cast may even show the marks where the muscles of the living animal were attached to the bone. Casts such as these are an important kind of fossil that paleontologists study. The Petrified Forest in Arizona is an area of more than 100 square miles (260 square kilometers), filled with stone casts of trees that lived long ages ago.

As the soil builds up year after year, and then the buried parts turn into rock, strata (layers) are formed. In cuts deep into the earth, such as the mile-deep Grand Canyon carved out by the Colorado River, these strata can clearly be seen as bands of different-colored rocks. Each stratum contains fossils of animals and plants that lived during the period when its soil was still uncovered.

The strata closest to the surface are usually most recent, and the deepest strata are usually oldest. Under your house there may be buried the foundation of a house built by frontier settlers, and beneath that the remains of an Indian camp. Still lower may be the bones of woolly mammoths, or even dinosaurs that roamed the lands long before there were any humans.

How can paleontologists tell how old fossils are? There are various ways. Scientists have measured the rate that soil builds up, and so the depth of the strata gives them a guide to the age. They can also use more sophisticated tests, such as determining the amounts of certain radioactive isotopes.

The fossils that have been found are only a very tiny fraction of all the animals and plants that have lived on our planet. And so the study of fossils is like trying to put together a giant jigsaw puzzle, of which most of the pieces are missing. Even so, scientists have learned a great deal about the story of life on earth.

This skull is 1.8 million years old. It was put together from 150 fragments of fossil bone.

A paleontologist does not need a whole skeleton to get a good idea of what an animal looked like. From a piece of a jawbone, he or she can figure out what the rest of the jaw must have looked like. The shape of the jaw will suggest things about the shape of the skull and the neck and shoulders. Working carefully with broken bits of skeletons, the paleontologist fills in the missing parts with clay. Markings on the fossil bones show where the muscles were attached, and layers of clay are added to reconstruct the muscles. With the shape of the muscles filled in, the expert knows how the skin and other tissues must have fit over them. Finally there is a model of how the animal looked when it was alive.

Through the study of bones, paleontologists have learned about the great dinosaurs that once ruled the earth. They have found traces of the first birds and followed the development of mammals from tiny, mouselike forms to apelike creatures who may have been the ancestors of the first people on earth.

The skeleton of the ornitholestes dinosaur (bottom), which lived about 138 million years ago, is 6 feet (1.8 meters) long. Note how it resembles the skeleton of the much smaller pigeon (top).

GLOSSARY

acromegaly—enlargement of the bones of the face, hands, and feet, caused by secretion of too much growth hormone.

appendicular skeleton—the bones of the appendages (limbs), suspended from the axial skeleton.

arthroscope—a fiber-optic probe used to see into joints and perform microsurgery.

axial skeleton—the central portion of the skeleton, consisting of the skull, backbone, and ribs.

backbone—the spine or vertebral column.

ball-and-socket joint—a joint in which a ball-shaped portion of a bone fits into a cup-shaped portion of another bone; permits free movement.

bone marrow—living material inside bone cavities, in which blood cells are formed.

bunion—bulging of the joint at the base of the big toe, due to inflammation of the joint and thickening of the bone.

bursa—fluid-filled sacs in joints, in places where tendons rub against bones. (Plural: bursae.)

bursitis—inflammation of the bursa in joints.

calcaneus—the heel bone.

callus—new growth of bone joining the broken ends of a fracture.

cancellous bone—spongy bone.

carpal bones—wrist bones.

carpal tunnel syndrome—inflammation of the tendons that run through channels in the wrist bones.

cartilage—gristly material at the ends of bones; also forms a baby's skeleton.

cementum—a hard substance that holds tooth roots in place.

cervical vertebrae—vertebrae in the neck; the upper seven vertebrae.

chiropractor—a health-care worker who manipulates the spine.

chitin—a tough, plasticlike material that forms an insect's exoskeleton.

clavicle—collarbone.

cleft palate—a birth defect in which there is an opening in the roof of the mouth due to failure of the maxillae to fuse during prenatal development.

coccyx—four fused vertebrae at the end of the spine; the "tailbone."

collagen—a tough protein fiber found in bones and connective tissue.

compact bone—the hard part of bone, just under the periosteum.

costal cartilage—strips of cartilage that attach the ribs to the sternum.

cranium—skull.

cuticle—an insect's exoskeleton.

dentin—bonelike substance that makes up most of the tooth.

diaphysis—the shaft of a long bone.

dislocation—slippage of a bone out of its joint.

enamel—hard substance that covers the crown of a tooth.

endoskeleton—internal skeleton.

epiphysis—the end portion of a long bone.

ergonomics—the science of designing furniture and tools that are comfortable and easy to use.

exoskeleton—an external skeleton; muscles are attached on the inside.

femur—thighbone.

fibula—the smaller bone in the lower leg.

forensic scientist—an expert who can deduce information about crimes and victims from the study of bones and other evidence.

fossil—the remains of an ancient creature, including stone casts of bones.

fracture—broken bone; in a simple fracture the broken ends do not pierce the skin; in a compound fracture the broken bone pierces the skin.

fulcrum—the pivot of a lever.

gliding joint—a joint permitting two bone surfaces to slide over each other to a limited degree.

gout—painful joints resulting from deposits of uric acid crystals.

hard palate—the roof of the mouth.

Haversian canals—microscopic channels in bone tissue.

hinge joint—a joint permitting back-and-forth motion.

humerus—upper arm bone.

ilium—one of the three bones that form the pelvis.

invertebrate—an animal without a backbone.

ischium—one of the three bones that form the pelvis.

joints—connections of bones.

kyphosis—excessive curvature of the upper part of the spine.

lever—a simple machine that multiplies the force applied.

ligaments—tough bands of tissue connecting bones.

lordosis—excessive curvature of the lower part of the spine.

lumbago—lower back pain due to back muscle or ligament strain.

lumbar vertebrae—vertebrae in the lower back; the first five after the thoracic vertebrae.

mandible—lower jaw.

matrix—the nonliving part of bone, containing minerals and protein fibers.

maxilla—upper jaw.

metacarpals—hand bones.

metatarsals—foot bones.

molting—shedding of an animal's outer covering, such as the exoskeleton.

orthodontics—a dental specialty dealing with correcting poor tooth alignment.

orthopedic surgeon—a specialist in the treatment of bone and joint problems.

ossification—bone formation; the replacement of cartilage by bone.

osteoarthritis—inflammation of the joints due to accumulated wear and tear.

osteoblast—bone-building cell.

osteoclast—bone-dissolving cell.

osteocytes—bone cells.

osteopath—a doctor who uses manipulation and massage to treat bone-related aches and pains.

osteoporosis—thinning of the bones with age.

paleontologist—a scientist who studies the remains of ancient creatures.

patella—kneecap.

pelvic girdle—the bony arch from which the leg bones are suspended.

pelvis—hipbones.

periosteum—membrane surrounding bone.

phalanges—finger or toe bones.

physical therapist—a health-care worker who applies heat, ice, massage, and/or supervised exercises to aid in restoring strength and motion to muscles and joints.

pivot joint—a joint permitting side-to-side rotation.

pubis—one of the three bones that form the pelvis.

radius—one of the forearm bones.

rheumatoid arthritis—inflammation of the joints due to an autoimmune reaction.

rib cage—the 12 pairs of ribs and the cavity they enclose.

rickets—softness and malformation of the bones due to mineral or vitamin D deficiency.

sacrum—the second five lumbar vertebrae, in the hip area; in adults they are usually fused into a single bone.

saddle joint—a saddle-shaped joint permitting considerable freedom of movement.

scapula—shoulder blade. (Plural: scapulae.)

sciatica—pain in the lower back and leg due to pressure of a slipped disk on the sciatic nerve.

scoliosis—sideways curvature of the spine.

sesamoid bones—small bones embedded in tendons of the knee, hand, and foot.

shoulder girdle—the clavicle and scapula, bones from which the arm bones are suspended.

skeletal muscles—muscles that work with bones of the skeleton.

slipped disk—dislocation of vertebrae in which the cartilage pads slip out of place and press on the spinal cord.

spina bifida—a birth defect in which a portion of the spinal cord protrudes through an opening in the vertebral column.

spinal canal—the channel running through the center of the vertebrae.

spine—the vertebral column; the central support of the skeleton, consisting of individual bones called vertebrae.

sprain—overstretching of the ligaments holding a joint together.

stem cell—cell in the bone marrow from which blood cells are formed.

sternum—breastbone.

sutures—immovable joints in which bones are fused together.

synovial fluid—the lubricating liquid in joints.

talipes—clubfoot; a malformation in which the foot is twisted out of shape or position.

tarsals—ankle bones.

tendons—tough bands of tissue connecting muscles to bones.

tennis elbow—inflammation of the tendons on the outside of the elbow joint.

thoracic vertebrae—vertebrae in the upper back; the twelve middle vertebrae.

tibia—shinbone.

TMJ (temporomandibular joint disorder)—aching of jaws and other discomfort due to misalignment of jaws, clenching or grinding of teeth.

traction—a device in which a weight pulls against muscles to keep bones aligned properly while healing.

ulna—one of the forearm bones.

vertebra—one of the bones of the spine. (Plural: vertebrae.)

vertebrate—an animal with a backbone.

wormian bones—small bones that help to fill spaces in the cranial sutures.

TIMELINE

INDEX